TRIBALS OF ORISSA

The Changing Socio-Economic Profile

Edited by

Prof. B.c. Ray

TRIBALS OF ORISSA
The Changing Socio-Economic Profile

Edited by
Prof. B.c. Ray

GYAN

ISBN: 978-81-212-0270-1(HB)
First Published,
Published, 2009
Published by

Gyan Publishing House
5, Ansari Road
Daryaganj, New Delhi-110002
Phone: 011-47034999, 9811692060
www.gyanbooks.com
E-mail: books@gyanbooks.com

Printed at: G. Print Process, Delhi.

Editorial

The work "Tribals of Orissa : The Changing Socio-Economic Profile" is the result of the joint efforts of eminent historians and scholars from other disciplines who contributed articles and participated in a seminar under the auspices of the Centre for Advanced Studies in History and Culture, Bhubaneswar.

This is one of the most informative and thought-provoking and helpful book and provides not only historical analysis but sociological and multi-disciplinary analysis of the tribal life of Orissa. It is indeed fascinating to those who desire to know transformation of the cultural and socio-economic life of those people.

The work through its articles is designed to stimulate constructive thought in this field and explore new frontiers and can be looked upon as an important source of useful materials on study and research on history, culture and socio-economic life.

The organization owes immense gratitude to these numerous contributors who participated in the seminar for exchange of ideas and cirticism.

My sincere thanks are due to Dr. H.K. Parija, Lecturer in History, Rajadhani College, Bhubaneswar and an active member of this organization for unstinted help in the compilation work.

We are very much grateful to the Indian Council of Social Science Research, New Delhi for sanctioning a grant for the publication of the work. The organization also records its high sense of gratitude to the Consultant, Professor A.K. Das, Director, Cultural Research Institute, Calcutta, whose suggestions and comments on several articles were extremely helpful for effecting some suitable changes to make the entire book better and more impressive.

B.C. RAY

Preface

Comparatively less work has so far been done in socio-economic life of the tribals of Orissa. Whatever has been done so far is mere anthropological study of some aspects not even a full sociological analysis. In order to analyse the action and interaction of both tribal and non-tribal culture of Orissa and to assess the changing pattern of the social life of tribals of Orissa, a seminar was organized at Bhubaneswar on 18th November 1984.

It was an academic gathering taking many eminent specialists from different disciplines. All what was aimed was to give an interdisciplinary approach for the assessment of so difficult a problem of socio-economic and cultural changes in tribals life of Orissa. The articles presented to this seminar were research works and on the spot observations and analysis were thoroughly discussed in the seminar. The discussions ranged from the mutual interactions of non-tribal and tribal culture, the absorption of serveral gods and goddesses from the tribal fold into the Hindu pantheon. Deliberations could however trace to what extent Hindu culture has been indebted to tribal culture and vice-versa. Again the segregated and isolated life of the tribals, in the hilly region shut off from the non-tribal belt, could retain many traditionally prejudicial superstitions and customs and practices which in later period particularly during the days of British rule, were found injurious to the progress of a better social life. Therefore they took measures against mariah, human sacrifice, and infanticide and the eradication of such social evils brought some social changes and the tribals previously left to their isolated life were disturbed and British Missionary activities in the tribal areas made the tribals to be acquainted with more about the outside world and better interchange of ideas broke their closed door policy. Yet the British, kept them in less isolated situation without any planned programme for their upliftment and integration with the non-tribal regions. It is only when India became free from the foreign yoke, that various plans and programmes could be worked out for their all possible improvements. Social, political, economic and cultural changes in their life style have been noticed because of the implementation of national programmes mostly financed by the Government of India. On the one hand care has been taken to allow them to develop their cultural traits, on the other hand possible facilities are provided to prepare ground for their integration with the national streams of India.

This is a very brief survey of the changing pattern of the socio-economic life of the tribals of Orissa and it is hoped that interested readers may find the work informative and useful as an effective study on tribals of Orissa.

B.C. RAY.

Director
Centre for Advanced
Studies in History and
Culture
Bhubaneswar.

Introduction

In a society there are changes in social life and it is more so in a progressive society because of the continuous actions and reactions of different forces and factors both internal and external. In a dynamic world, social changes shall have to come in some form or other, perceptible or imperceptible in spite of any resistance for assimilation. There are changes also in cultural evolution even if it may be slow, because the religious practices, the people performed in ancient period are not exactly the same as we are performing today, though outwardly to a superficial observer they appear to be the same. Because of the influence of the age, the old socio-religious concept is receiving a new dimension taking into consideration, the present need and dynamic situation. Even in the evolution of art and sculputure and architecture, the same principle is noticed when observed minutely.

In the same way changes are noticed in the socio-economic life of the tribals of Orissa. For assessment of such social problems as "The changing pattern of the socio-economic life of the tribals of Orissa" as a particular discipline like history was not considered enough, an interdisciplinary method as found applied generally in France and in the U.S.A. has been applied. The combined efforts of Historians, Anthropologists, psychologists, economists and even literary-critics etc. have been made to bring a more balanced and favourable atmosphere to get a full picture of the changing society in different aspects with a view to finding out a solution for the problem, the soceity is confronting.

Here there is an attempt to review the tribal life of Orissa in the context of economic improvement and social changes. Since the Aryanization of this land now called Orissa the process of change in some form or other directly or indirectly has affected the tribals who preferred to keep their distinct culture and social life in tact, being segregated in the hilly regions of Orissa. The regions of Koraput, Mayurbhanj, Phulbani and Sundargarh districts are more inhabited by the larger number of tribals than any other districts of Orissa. Survey shows that in India there are 427 Scheduled Tribes with different socio-economic spectrum. Out of them 62 are in Orissa. The Khonds of Orissa alone are the seventh largest tribal group in India and they are twice the size of the better known Naga people of Assam. In number and group the tribal population is significant here, because the population in miserly calculation goes beyond 50 lakhs. It is said "Orissa can be proud of her wealth in the form of tribal people because she stands first among all the States in India by the size of the Scheduled Tribes population which constitutes about 24.07% of the total population of the State and 14.2% of the tribal population of India."

A conspicuous change was noticed in the life of the tribals during the British rule in those sectors, where the Christianity penetrated. Change in religious faith led to corresponding change in festivals and village organization. Such transformation indicated the process of compromise, combination and elimination and conflict among two types of traditions, indigenous and borrowed. Borrowed Christianity, originated, developed and flourished, was successful in introducing modernised style of life in certain section of tribal villages breaking the cultural homogeneity of the tribals.

Tribal villages of Orissa divided in terms of their ecological, economic and cultural development have been differently affected by modern process of change. These villages are found to have often different types of economic organizations and economic problems which need to be considered in the light of their cultural characteristics and age-old traditions. In many cases cultural traditions stand in the way of economic changes. However, with accelerating impact of urbanization and industrialization, agricultural economy is surely but slowly undergoing transformation.

Constitutional provisions, plan and programme, rise of local leadership, industrialization and urbanization have impact for change in life with the diversion of economy from agriculture to non-agriculture, a lot of changes in social spheres of tribal people have been brought about. These changes are markedly found in traditional activities, participation in the dance and other cultural activities, dresses and food habits and even the role of social leadership.

With the rise of many factories in many Adivasi areas, spread of education and impact of ideas from outside world, there is a remarkable change in their outlook, in their world view value, attitude system and above all in the very philosophy of life. It seems as if the very traditional culture marked with homogeneity, simplicity, and cooperation and leisurely life have been shaken.

The level of aspiration and lust for material comfort seems to be increasing indicating the sense of individualism and lack of love for traditional code of conduct and social taboos are apparent among the emerging urban industrial oriented Adivasi communities.

The modern processes by and large have put up before the tribals, the Western-Urban-Industrial-Democratic model for inducing transformation. With the operation of those factors of change, the culture of the tribals is in flux and cultural heterogeneity is reflected in all aspects of their life. Numerous tribal communities are affected by this change.

Thus socio-economic cultural changes are certain continuing phenomena. The same is true in the tribal life of Orissa, though the changes in their socio-economic field are not what is to be expected in the terms of national standard.

The problems, the tribals in Orissa, as in other parts of India, face are many which are in a sense traditional, hereditary and are due to their love for isolation, exclusiveness and avoidance of contact with non-tribals. Some of such problems may be cited here.

Most of the tribals in Orissa are dependent on agriculture holdings which are small, scattered and uneconomic. The income from such primitive type of agriculture is meagre. As a result they are kept below poverty line.

The method they adopt in the shifting cultivation known as *podu* or *dangara chasa* is to select a patch of the hilly region every year, clean the forest slopes, burn the fallen trees and bushes, prepare the field in broad ash-covered soild for cultivation.

The agricultural or forest products whatever are collected by tribals and procured by the businessmen at a very cheap rate. As a result, they fail to acquire sufficient necessaries of life in return of the products they sell.

The income from this primitive agricultural technique is quite inadequate to fulfil their social obligations and rituals. So they look for economic relief from other sources. Large number of tribal families, therefore, borrow money from the crafty money-lenders. As the borrowed money is spent for non-productive purposes, they remain indebted. So it is said that the "tribals are born in debt, live in debt and die in debt".

Another way of meeting their expenditure-demand is to do bonded labour. This system of bonded labour has emerged from indebtedness and is known as *Goti* or *Helia* in Orissa. According to this system, the tribal pledges his person against a loan. He has to work as required by his creditor. He is not to be released until he is to repay his loan. Some families work in their master's house even for generations.

Besides, the want of education and non- removal of the age-old prejudices and love for isolated life in inaccessible region and unwillingness to establish relation with the advanced non-tribal people, do not help them to create a congenial enviornment for economic growth.

Again their lack of adaptability to the changing ecological environment and national forest policy for harnessing the natural resources and industrial programmes, bring before them fresh economic problems which, by their traditional and conservative outlook, they are not able to solve.

As a result their economic condition deteriorates. Since independence, specific provisions are provided in the constitution of India for the protection and all-round development of the tribals, so that they would fall in line with the mainstream of life in India. Both central and state governments have taken steps for socio-economic and educational development of the tribals. Vast amount of money is being spent in this direction. The Tribal and Rural welfare Department, has established many Chatasalis, Sevashrams and High Schools for educating tribals. But, this anti-illiteracy campaign has not proved so much successful as according to a Census report the percentage of literacy has increased, from 7.4% in 1961 to 9.5% in 1971 only.

In the economic field the establishment of the Tribal Development Cooperative Corporation of Orissa Ltd., is considered an important step.

It is meant for providing advances for production-cum-consumption loans to the tribals and is supposed to check the exploitation of the tribals by private traders and middlemen. But, the society is not able to compete with the cunning traders and middlemen. Also the tribals themselves find that the cumbersome procedure adopted by the society for granting loan is not suitable to them. So the problem of tribal indebtedness is not solved.

So far as the suggestions for remedies are concerned, even for economic uplift, there is need for spread of education in the tribal sectors, as a liberal education, will help in taking away the barrier between the tribal and non-tribal sector, remove the cultural isolation and will provide field for free cultural intercourse between tribal and non-tribal areas, also will help in bringing a spirit of competition, which may perhaps be basic ground for economic uplift. But the education system will be such as will inculcate in the mind of the tribals, a sense of inspiration, confidence and benefit.

The persons involved in such educational agency should render duties under a special programme.

In implementing the governmental programmes, adequate attention should be paid to the anti-exploitation measures. Elimination of indebtedness should be an important point.

Provisions for credit facilities should be made through the cooperative society for the purchase of consumer needs as salt, kerosene and coarse cloth etc.

So also marketing facilities should be provided to the tribals for sale of such articles as tamarind,mahua and broom-stick and sabai grass etc., as available in the forest regions, where tribals live.

There should be demonstrations of the improved agricultural practices in tribal areas and efforts should be made to persuade them to take advantage of modern agricultural benefits, so that the primitive system of agriculture will be gradually replaced by more improved one.

To provide occupational opportunities, there is also need for development of cottage and small scale industries in the tribal scctor where necessary. In selection of the types of industries, such industries are to be promoted, as will be beneficial and befitting to their social and natural environment.

The forest department should create some employment opportunities for the tribals rather than merely mechanically enforcing the legal rights over the tribals. Such legalistic approach will create misunderstanding, which in turn might develop a sense of separatist tendency in the minds of the tribals.

The best way for having free cultural intercourse between the tribals and non-tribals, is to provide adequate transportation and communication facilities. Roads should be constructed to the inaccessible tribal regions. This will not only bring educative value, but also improve the commercial and economic base of the tribal area. But at the same time, adequate precautions should be taken against the exploitation of the tribals from the hands of the unscrupulous businessmen, who because of easy communication would swarm to these regions to procure the forest products at a considerably cheap rate by any means from the hands of simple-minded tribal people.

Whatever plans and programmes are executed for the uplift of the economic condition of the tribals, much depends, on the sincerity and honesty of the officials, who are on the scene. One of the problems which often arises in implementing programme is want of adequate supervising agency to supervise the works done at the bottom level. If there is constant supervision and pressure from the high level to see that the work is done according to plan, much may be saved in terms of money and human energy.

Whatever might be the measures adopted for the problems of the tribals, the inevitable process of change in the tribal sectors has set in. The impact of science and technology and the access of modern man to the hitherto-inaccessible tribal regions utilization of forest resources and hilly regions, the abodes of tribals, for implementation of national programmes, harnessing of mineral resources for country's upliftment, establishment of various factories in periphery of secluded hilly belts, have already created a completely new atmosphere never known to the tribals. This has given them perhaps a new incentive to turn their faces to the new life in front. Forces of modernization are active. Industrialization, perhaps, an effective means of acculturation of diverse people, has affected the socio-economic life of the tribals.

This has again raised the question how to preserve the cultural self-image of the tribals. Problem is, on the one hand, the tribal cultural identity is to be maintained and on the other hand, it is a duty to widen the economic and political frontier for integration into the Indian national stream. Of course industrialization has already, at many places. brought the process. But the time for achievement of the goal depends on the adaptability and response of the triblas to this new challenge and the congenial environmental factors arising out of well-thought out national programmes executed judiciously and tactfully. The tribal cultural identity will stand as in case of other cultural groups of India, on the principle of diversity in unity, the basic theme of Indian national life.

B.C. RAY

Director
Centre for Advanced
Studies in History
and Culture
Bhubneswar

Contributing Authors

1. Dr. H.K. Parija
   Lecturer in History,
   Rajadhani College,
   Bhubaneswar
2. A.K. Rath
   Reader in History,
   Khallikote College,
   Berhampur
   Orissa
3. Dr. L.K. Panda
   Reader in History,
   Dhenkanal College,
   Dhenkanal
4. M.M. Mohapatra
   Lecturer in History,
   Khallikote College,
   Berhampur
   Orissa
5. Dr. N.K. Behura,
   Department of Anthropology
   Utkal university,
   Bhubaneswar
   &
   K.K. Mishra
   Dept. of Anthropology,
   University of Hyderabad,
   Hyderabad

6. Dr. Mohan Lal Sahoo
Lecturer in Oriya
Banki College,
P.O. Banki
Dist. Cuttack
7. Dr. Fakir Mohan Sahoo, Ph. D. (Queen's),
Reader in Psychology,
Centre of Advanced Studies in Psychology,
Utkal University,
Vani Vihar,
Bhubaneswar
8. Dr. Dandapani Behera
Head of Department of History,
Bhanja Nagar College,
Bhanja Nagar,
Dist. Ganjam
9. Shri Bhagaban Sahu,
Lecturer in History,
Vishmagiri College
Orissa
10. Dr. N.P. Mohapatra
Medical Officer (Eye Specialist)
District Headquarters Hospital,
Keonjhar
11. J.P. Kuanr
Reader in Anthropology,
Department of Anthropology,
Khallikote College
Berhampur
Orissa
&
S. Patel
Reader,
Government College, Phulbani
Phulibani
12. Dr. Basudev Sahoo
Professor of Economics,
Revenshaw College,
Cuttack
&

Ajay Kumar Mohapatra
Lecturer in Economics,
Government College,
Angul

13. Dr. U.C. Mohanty,
Reader, Department of Anthropology,
University of Madras

Contents

1

ARYANIZATION OF TRIBAL DEITY— THE JAGANNATH

Dr. H.K. Parija*

The origin and antiquity of Lord Jagannath, the Lord of the Universe, is shrouded in considerable mystery. We have no positive evidences to know how and when the god came to be worshipped at Puri and became one of the prominent deities of Hindu pantheon. It is also difficult to know whether the god was an Aryan deity or a tribal deity later on Aryanized due to the mingling of the Aryan and non-Aryan cultures. An attempt has been made in this paper to find out the antiquity of Lord Jagannath as a tribal deity, who later on was Aryanized.

According to the tradition recorded in the Utkala Khanda[1] of the 'Skanda Purana' Indradyumna, the ruler of Avanti in the Satya Yuga and a great votary of Lord Visnu, sent Vidyapati, the brother of his family priest, to Odradesa to locate the exact place where Lord Nilamadhava (Visnu) was worshipped secretly. Coming to Odradesa Vidyapati took shelter in a Sabara village, very near to the Blue Mountain (Nilasaila). Winning over the friendship of the Sabara chief

*Lecturer in History, Rajadhani College, Bhubaneswar.

Visvavasu and marrying his daughter Lalita, Vidyapati was able to see Lord Nilamadhava. After tracing the route to the shirne of Nilamadhava, Vidyapati went back to Avanti to inform his sovereign Lord Indradyumna the whereabouts of Lord Nilamadhava. The king, accompanied by Narada, set out for Odradesa to pay homage to the Lord. But at the boundary of the country he came to know about the miraculous disappearance of the Lord. He became extremely sad. Narada consoled him that the Lord would appear in the form of a 'Daru' (sacred wood). A few days after, Lord Nilamadhava Himself appeared in a dream to Indradyumna. The next day the king and his attendants brought the "Daru" from the sea-shore and placed in on the Mahavedi with respect.

As directed by the Lord in the dream, Indradyumna ordered for fashioning beautiful images out of the sacred "Daru". But strangely no carpenter was available. At last Visvakarma, the Divine Builder, appeared in the guise of an old carpenter and agreed to build the images on the condition that he be allowed to remain undisturbed inside the temple for twenty one days. As days passed on the sound of the carpenter's tools became thinner and thinner and when no sound was heard Queen Gundicha became impatient and curious. On her insistence when the doors of the temple were opened no carpenter was found inside and the images of Jagannath, Balabhadra and Subhadra were found incomplete.

This legend with slight variations is also mentioned in the Brahma Purana[2] as well as in the Oriya Mahabharata[3] of Sarala Das. Very interestingly this Indradyumna legend associating the Sabaras with the Lord Nilamadhava (Jagannath) is also supported by epigraphic and historical evidences. The Sabaras, who belonged to the proto-Austrolaid tribe, were the worshippers of tree in the Vindhyarange and Mahendragiri from the earliest times. They were the worshippers of the Sthanumurti[4] (a branchless trunk) which in course of time replaced the primitive tree worship. Later on this worship of the Sthanumurti seems to have mingled with the worship of the God Purusottama-Visnu. In the Rigveda[5] there is a passage which refers to the Lord of Daru (*Adojad*

Daru plavate Sindhohpare apurusam). According to the fourteenth century Vedic commentator Sayana[6] A.D (1300-1380 this Daru represents the wooden image of Purusottama. This view is also supported by a fifteenth century tradition as recorded in the Kondavidu copper plate[7] grant of Ganadeva of the time of Gajapati Kapilendradeva. According to this tradition Jagannath resembles the log of wood as spoken of in the Sruti (*Sa bhagavan shrutyukta daru akrtih*). The Sabaras worshipped a deity named Kitung who had ten synonyms. One of those familiar synonyms was Jaganta or Jaganelo.[8] The Sabaras who were the worshippers of Jaganta made of wood, were also devout worshippers of Madhava, the predecessor of Lord Jagannath, according to another tradition recorded in the Skanda Purana.[9] This lead us to believe that Lord Jaganta of the Savaras in course of time was converted into the Aryan God Jagannath, who is no other than Madhava or Krsna. With the gradual Aryanization the Sabaras were influenced by the Brahmanical form of Hinduism and incorporated the principles of Brahmanism in their socioreligious life.

In this connection there is a very interesting tradition recorded in the Vizagapatnam plates[10] of Anantavarman Chodagangadeva of the year A.D. 1119 This tradition says that king Kamarnava, conquered the Mahendragiri region towards the close of the fifth century A.D., acknowledged a tribal deity of the Sabara tribe as Siva-Gokarnesvara and worshipped it as the tutelary deity (*ista devata*) of the family. Bestowed with grace by the Lord, Kamarnava climbed down the mountain, killed the chief of the Savara tribe and conquered Kalinga. This tradition speaks of the Aryanisation of a tribal deity, which was due to the migration of the Vedic Brahmins from North to other parts of India and the spread of the Aryan culture. A verse in the Bhagavata Purana[11] informs us that the Kiratas, the Hunas, the Pulindas, the Abhiras and other tribal people were influenced by the worship of Lord Visnu. This process of intermingling of the Aryan and non-Aryan cultures led to the Aryanization of many tribal deities.

It is very interesting to note a lot of similarities between the renewal of tribal ritual of the post, representing Stambheswari or Khambhesvari and the Navakalevara ritual of Lord Jagannath at Puri. According to the tradition followed in the Jagannath temple during Navakalevara. the Patimahapatra,[12] head of the half-savara Brahmins and the descendant of Brahmin Vidyapati and Savara Lalita, who leads the party of the Daitas* to find out the Daru for the Four Deities and goes to Kakatapur, is told in a dream by Goddess Mangala the exact location and the appearance of the Darus. In case of the renewal of the tribal deity Stambhesvari the goddess Herself appears in a dream through the medium of the priest called *Bhejini*[13] and indicates the spot where the tree is to be found. The tree to be selected must display certain features which are similar in both the cases. In case of the tribal custom the new tree, before being cut off, is worshipped with the sacrifice of a sheep or a goat and the first stroke on the tree is always performed by the Dehuri, Chief priest of the tribal deity. In case of the Daru of Lord Jagannath the sacrificial ritual is symbolically performed and the first stroke is performed by the chief priest called Acharya.[14] In both the cases the tree should fall to the east and should not touch the ground in any case. The tradition that the logs should be carried in a special cart exclusively pulled by human hands and should not touch the ground is followed in both the cases. The carvings of the images of Puri temple is done by carpenters in a closed room and nobody except the Daitas and Pati Mahapatra are allowed to enter the place where the figures are being carved. The carpenters are to lead a pure life and observe certain rituals during this period. In case of the tribal custom the carpenter is to obstain from drinks and drugs and to lead a pure life.[15] Just as the sacred Daru is inserted into the Puri images before their consecration, five metals (gold, silver, iron, copper and brass) are inserted into the "Post" of the tribals before it is consecrated.

Moreover, the images of Jagannath, Balabhadra and Subhadra at the Puri temple are crude and have "a tribal look".[16] The post, representing Stambhesvari is also crude

*Savaras who were the descendants of Visvavasu.

and sometimes the figure of Nrusimha (an aspect of Jagannath) is carved on the post in a very crude form.

All these similarities between the Puri Navakalevara ritual and that of the tribal deity Stambhesvari lead us to suggest a close link between the Hindu God Jagannath and the tribal deity.

The Sabaras also play a distinct role in the daily worship of Lord Jagannath at Puri. A special group of priests, the Daitas (descendents of the Sabara chief Visvevasu, the first worshipper of Jagannath in the hoary past), who are called the relatives of Lord Jagannath, is entrusted with many important services. During the Anavasara[17] (sickness of the deities) veremony of the deities, it is not the Brahmanas but the Daitas who take-up the worship. During this period the Vedic offerings and rituals are stopped.

The Daitas also play important roles at the outset of the Car festival. During this period the deities are worshipped not in Vedic lines but in tribal lines. Even the deities are dressed in the Sabara costume. Moreover, as Dr. K.C. Mishra[18] points out very rightly—"The deities move towards the cars in north-west (isna) direction whereas in Aryan process, the procession moves towards eastern direction. Hence, the north-west movement of the deities towards the cars, obviously points to the impact of the Sabara convention on the festival.

Since the Daitas (Savaras) claim Jagannath as a member of their family, they sit together with the Lords and take the "Gyantisara" (the dishes taken by members of the same family together). As descendents of Lord Jagannath the Daitas claim on the articles used by the deceased Jagannath after Navakalevara. After disposing of the old figures the Daitas take bath and observe mourning because of the death of one of their clan. They weep and cry for the death of Jagannath and for ten days remain in a state of ritual impurity, observing all sorts of obsequies prescribed in the Hindu Dharmasastra. On the tenth day they cut their hairs and nails, shave their body and take purificatory bath in the Markandeya tank.

The very fact that the Daitas (Sabaras) even today consider lord Jagannath as a member of their clan and observe all sorts of obsequies, is a clear proof of the tribal origin of Lord Jagannath.

Thus, tradition as well as present practices very clearly indicate the tribal origin of Lord Jagannath. But how the tribal deity Nilamadhava came to Puri to be worshipped as Lord Jagannath is a mystery, which is yet to be solved. Lord Jagannath is a synthesis between the Aryan and non-Aryan cultures.

REFERENCES

1. Skanda Purana, Chs. 6, 7, 9 and 15.
2. Brahma Purana, Ch. 45, slokas 71-76.
3. Mahabharata (111), Ch. 198, sloka (1)
4. See line 7 of the Buguda Plates of Madhavaraja (11), 9. C Vol. (1), pt (11), p. 167.
5. Rgveda (X), 155.3.
6. Rgveda with Sayana's commentary, edited by Vaidika Samsodhana Mandal, Poona, Vol IV, p. 841.
7. I.A., Vol. XX, p. 391.
8. Mishra, Dr. K.C., The Cult of Jagannath, Calcutta, 1971, p. 18.
9. Skanda Purana, Visnu Khanda, (Purusottama Mahatmya), Ch. VII, Vrs. 85, 97.
10. Rajguru, Dr. S.N., History of the Ganges, Vol. II, p. 14f.
11. Bhagavat Purana, II, 4.18.
12. Tripathy, G.C. Navakalevara in The Cult of Jagannath and the Regional Traditions of Orissa, Eschmann, Kulke and Tripathy (Eds), pp. 231-232.

13. Eschmann, A. Prototypes of Navakalevara Ritual, in Ibid., p. 268.
14. Ibid., p. 270.
15. Ibid., pp. 269-270.
16. Eschmann, A. The Vaisnava Typology of Hinduization and the origin of Jagannath, Ibid., p. 99.
17. Tripathy, G.C., Navakalevara, Ibid., p. 224.
18. Mishra, Dr. K.C., The cult of Jagannath, Calcutta, 1971, p. 96.

2

ARYANIZED TRIBAL GODDESSES IN THE DISTRICT OF GANJAM

A.K. Rath*

A host of formless aboriginal goddesses in the Ganjam district of Orissa such as Stambhesvari (Khambesvari) of Aska, Vyaghradevi of Kullada, 7 kms. to the north of Bhanjanagara, Ratanei of Kesaripalli near Kendupadara, Kandhuni of Sorada, Narayani of Konkorada, Samalai (Saunlei near Hinjilicut, Tara-Tareni near Purushottamapur, Narayani on the Bhaleri hills to the north-west of Khalikote opposite the Chilka lake, Kandhuni to the north of Chatrapur on the old National Highway, Mahuri Kalua at Kankia, Bhairavi at Mantridi and the Budhi Thakurani the presiding deity of Berhampur town have undergone the process of Aryanisation through ages of history, consequent upon the interaction between the Brahmanical and tribal cultures. These aboriginal goddesses, originally worshipped by the Khonds, Savaras and other tribal people, have played an important role in the folk religion and the regional cultural tradition of Ganjam, nay of the southern part of Orissa. The Aryan invaders who had settled amidst the tribes incourse of time adopted and worshipped these Goddesses in order to enjoy the confidence and seek the cooperation of the

*Reader in History, Khallikote College, Berhampur.

latter in their settlements. So much so gradually these goodesses were aryanised or hinduised being transformed from a formidable nomadic or tribal cult into sakti cult and worshipped both by the Aryan and the non-Aryan sections of the society.

This process of transformation was made by the Aryan invaders, who, in the meantime, had split up themselves into severe ruling dynasties, established kingdoms of their own and ruled over the tribals. They depended upon the tribals not only for the consolidation and expansion but also for the security of internal communication and borders of their newly established kingdoms. The Aryan kings also felt the necessity of procuring the lands of the tribals and their services for the promotion and extension of agriculture which would yield enough surplus crops to meet the expenses of the royal establishment as well as the army. Besides, from the military point of view the service of the sturdy tribals were essential for the defence of their kingdoms. Therefore, the Aryan chiefs always sought the support and loyalty of the tribals and kept them in good humour by a gradual process of the inclusion of the tribal groups into the Hindu caste system by adoption and absorption of some aspects of their religion and culture into the Aryan fold, for example, they aryanised and patronised and the tribal Goddeses as their family or tutelary deity which enabled them to stabilize their political power and its legitimation in the Hindu tribal zone of Ganjam.

In this gradual process of Aryanization and patronage of the tribal goddesses the Brahmanas played an important role who defined and codified the duties of the tribes, which as the Mahabharata puts it, "reside in the dominion of the Aryan kings". According to the Mahabharata they should lead a "recluse living in the forest...and serve their king...dig wells, give water to the thirsty travellers, give away bed and other reasonable presents upon Brahmanas".[1] These Brahmanas who were donated rent-free villages in the remote areas, had to perform the duty of propagating this ideal for the sake of themselves as well as their kings. Thus Prof. R.S. Sharma has rightly stated that "the significance of land grant to Brahmanas is no difficult to appreciate. The grantees brought new knowledge which improved cultivation and inculcated in the aborigines a sense of loyalty to the established order upheld by the rulers".[2] The Brahmanas who settled in forest tracts through rent-free land grants came into contact with the tribals and with whose help they could cultivate their lands.[3] Gradually there developed harmony amongst the Brahmanas and the forest tribes which led to the interaction of their respective cultures. So much so mother Goddesses worshipped by the non-Aryan tribes entered the Brahmanical pantheon[4]. In course of time they were aryanized and transformed into Sakti Cult.

The aboriginal origin of these Goddesses is suggested by the horrible practice involving human sacrifices. The Yupas or sacrificial posts infront of the temple of these goddesses bear testimony to this practice. None of these Goddesses who are mothers, has a male consort. This indicates their origin in the matriarchical society and thereby proves their aboriginal origin.[5] It may be mentioned here that the *Marhabharata, Harivamsa* and *Kubjika tantra* and *Varangacharita*[7] refer to the worship of these mother Goddesses by the non-Aryan tribes. The *Kalika Purana,* significantly enough, forbids a Brahmana to make offerings of blood and flesh from his own body though the same is allowed to other castes. This evidently suggests the aboriginal character of the mother goddesses[8] In *Kalika Purana* we come across the *Savaras* as the worshippers of the mother Goddesses. Pargiter has stated that "the Aryans met with the religious practices and beliefs among whom they ruled over or came into lasting contact with and have assimilated some of them gradually thus modifying their own religion to a certain extent"[9]. This gives us an idea of how the Hindu religion became a blending of heterogeneous cults embodying the precepts of different tribes in different times.

The forests and hill tribes who believed in matriarchy were worshippers of Sakti. This explains why the abodes of autochthonous goddesses are found in the hill tracts or at least in tribal surroundings. The idea of female energy (Sakti) as the agent of creation led to the evolution of guardian spirits as cult goddesses in most tribal societies. Stambhesvari (Khambesvari,) Vyaghradevi and Tara-Tarini are the best examples of the many such aboriginal cult Goddesses of the Ganjam district of Orissa which underwent the process of aryanisation. They are concrete instances of the metamorphosis of totemdivines into cult goddesses. These deities do not possess any specific iconographic features, nor do they appear in all Indian Brahmanical theology. However, it is said that they "were acknowledged as members of the documented theology of the society in whose contact the tribes lived"[10]. Worshipped in the from of stones these deities have been anthropomorphised and converted into images. Most of these Goddesses were kept in open space under the bushy groves or under a tree on the road sides or hutments in them middle of the village or at one end or in the close vicinity of the village in the caves. But in course of time temples were also constructed to install these goddesses. The tribals had a conviction that sacrifices were essential to please the Goddesses. Hence animal and human sacrifices were offered to them. That is why the temples of these goddesses are generally found at secluded or lonely places.

In most of the temples of these aboriginal goddesses in the Ganjam district, as elsewhere, stones or pebbles are worshipped along with the main image in the sanctum sanctorum to which *Gandha* (sandal paste), *Pushpa* (flower) *Dhupa* (incense), *Dipa* (lamp), rice, fruits and vegetables are offered. Sometimes *Snana* (bath) is also offered. Goat, sheep and cocks are sacrificed before the goddess round the year, preferably on the *Sankranti* day, *Dasahara* and more ceremoniously in the months of *Chaitra* and *Asvina* to fulfil a desire. The priests, both males and famales, of these temples are not Brahmins. They are affiliated to different tribal groups. The male priests call themselves *Sudra Muni, Muni, Jani, Mali, Dehuri, Devata, Raula, Suara,* while the female priests are generally known as *Janiani*, *Naliani* and the like. The *puja* is performed in some temples everyday and in some others only once in a week, i.e., on Tuesday or Thursday or Saturday.

It is believed that these tribal goddesses protect human beings, cure diseases, save the tribes from the attack of ferocious wild animals, epidemics such as pox and cholera and ascertain fertility. The Khonds, Savaras and other aboriginal hill tribes believed that their goddesses cause famine as punishments for their sins. Therefore they feared to commit a sinful act. They also believed that their goddesses were unconquered and although they were the sources of all evils, they could confer every form of mundane benefit. Besides, they thought that the goddesses appeared on earth to restore peace and introduced the art of agriculture as well as other blessings into the world.[11]

Khambesvari, 'Goddess of the post or pillar', was originally worshipped by the hill tribes and their rulers of western Orissa and the Ghumusar region of the Ganjam district of Orissa. Her first royal patron was Tushtikara who ruled over the Kalahandi, Baudh and Ghumsar regions in the 5th or 6th century A.D. He has styled himself as Stambhesvari Pada Bhakta in his Terasingha copper plates[12] which reveals that king Tushtikara in order to cure his ailing mother, *Sri Sobhini* worshipped the feet of Goddess Stambhesvari the *Ista Devi* of his family. In the Ghumsar region at Aska on the bank of the river Rishikulya there is a temple of Khambesvari, the only of its kind in the Ganjam district. The area around the temple is called *Khambesvaripatana*. It is interesting to note that some of the place names mentioned in the Terasinga copper plates have been located by S.M. Rajguru[13] in the Aska region. In view of this it may be suggested that the Goddess *Khambesvari* at Aska was originally enshrined by Tushtikara in c. 5th/6th century A.D.

Khambesvari was also the tutelary deity of the Sulki royal family[14] (c. A.D. 600-800) of *Kodalakamandala* (Dhenkanal-Talcher region) and the Bhanja dynasty in the 9th century A.D. in Khinjilimandala[15] (Sonepur, Baud and Ghumsar regions). Under the patronage of the Bhanjas the worship of Khambesvari became very popular in the Ghumsar region as revealed by their inscriptions. The Kamalpur copper plate grant of the reign of Karnadeva[16] records the grant of the village Vadakela situated in the Mandala of Kulada in the Ghumsar region by Ranaka Sri Jayarnnama who claimed to have received boons from Goddess Khambesvari, a claim which is also made by the Bhanja rulers of Ghumsar. Jayarnnama might be a Bhanja feudatory of the Somavamsi king Karnadeva (c.A.D. 1100-1110), who worshipped Goddess Khambesvari at Aska. The later Bhanja kings of Ghumsar in the 17th century A.D. regarded Khambesvari at Aska as the presiding deity of the southern gate (Dakshina Dvara) of their kingdom.[17]

It is suggested[18] that the representation of Stambhesvari was probably made out on a Stambha (pillar) indicating a Siva Linga. Such a Linga with the representation of Sakti is no doubt found among the sculptural remains of eastern India[19]. It should however, be pointed out that whatever may have been the form of the Goddess worshipped by Tushtikara, the Sulkis and the Bhanjas, the deity is still adorned by the people of different castes of the Ganjam district under the prakritic name Khambesvari and in the form of a post on pillar[20]. Therefore, the work Stambhesvari seems to indicate that it is the 'Goddess of the pillar' without any special association with the Siva Linga. This pillar deity was so named by the Brahmana donees who knew Sanskrit and were responsible for Aryanising this aboriginal deity and transforming it into Sakti Cult.

An interesting legend[21] of the Khambesvari temple at Aska says that once Goddess Khambesvari appeared in a dream before Khambamuni who lived in the forest and desired that she should be worshipped by the latter. As per the wishes of Khambamuni she lived in his hut as his daughter. But this caused suspicion among the people passing nearby who did not like that an old man should should live in the company of a beautiful girl. Therefore, Khambamuni revealed the true self of the girl (Khambesvari), who convinced the people of the truth disclosed by the former by miraculously disappearing form the spot. From thence forward she made lot of fun and frolic with Khambamuni. Once she appeared before him holding in her arms a baby cut into pieces. Khambamuni could not tolerate such a sight and out of rage slapped her as a result of which her face turned to one side. After this incident she declared that her childhood play (Balya-lila) or 'disguise' was over, that her foster father (Khamamuni) would die and that she would be worshipped on the spot, i.e., in the forest by the tribal people. Yet another legend says that a Khond king used to worship eight tribal Goddesses called Khidsing among whom Khambesvari was one. Once in the form of a log of wood (Daru) she was carried by the floods of Rishikulya. A washerman caught hold of the log and while cutting it into pieces for the purpose of fuel blood came out of it. A few days after the washerman died. Later on Khambamuni or Sudramui saw the log in a dream and installed the Goddess Khambesvari under a tree in the form of wood.[22] But at present we find the image of Khambesvari at Aska in the form of a stone pole inside the temple whereas in front of the main door stands a wooden pole of about one meter high presiding over the sacrificial pit. The priests of the temple say that the wooden pole was the original log worshipped by the Khond king. Sacrifices are offered to the wooden pole and not to the main image. At the time of sacrifice the main door of the temple is closed so that it would not be visible to the main image.

Thus the wooden pole retains its aboriginal character, while the main image (Stone pole) inside the temple represents its Aryanised form. Thus the legends account for the affiliation of the tribals to the Goddess Khambesvari. The features of the baby cut into pieces, blood coming out of the log when it was cut convey the idea of human sacrifices or at least tantric practices associated with the Goddess. Further the Goddess appearing in a dream before Khambamuni in the forest and her desire to be worshipped in the forest, all indicate its aboriginal character.

Thus the Goddess Khambesvari at Aska is worshipped

both as an image in the Garbhagriha and as a wooden pole presiding over the sacrificial pit in front of the main image opposite the main door of the sanctum. The main image consists of a stone pole which has been anthropomorphised by the addition of a disk as head. Her nose and mouth are slightly carved. Her three eyes and the protruding tongue are made of gold. Her face is painted from time to time with a thick layer of pasty vermilion. In her eyes also found a layer of Kajjala (collyrium). She has been adorned with gorgeous silken dress and heavy golden ornaments. "Her image confers both, the impression of a real Hindu image, whose body and limbs are mostly not to be seen bacause of the dresses and ornaments and the impression of a pole, whose form is still evident in spite of the dress".[23] Some scholars have suggested that the figure of Khambesvari at Aska resembles the figure of Subhadra of the Holy Triad (Jagannatha, Balabhadra and Subhadra) of Puri, as both are similar in their iconography as well as iconology. As the worship of Khambesvari is known since the 5th or the 6th century A.D. it is said that her Hinduised iconography might be taken as the prototype for the development which led to the Subhadra figure of Puri.[24]

The priests of the Khambesvari temple are Sudras who have a tribal origin. In the past the priests were known as Sudramunis. But the present generation of the priests prefer to call themselves as Muni only, omitting the term Sudra apparently with a view to making their tribal or low-caste origin less known and thereby have elevated their social status. Animal sacrifices are offered to the Goddess on festive occasions like Dussehra and Tuesdays of the month of Chaitra. The non-vegetarian food (Bhoga) cooked by the Sudra priests is taken by all the devotees irrespective of caste.

Vyaghradevi, the Goddess of the Khonds or Kuis and the Savaras of Ghumsar, underwent the process of Aryanization under the patronage of the Bhanja ruling house of Ghumsar since the early medieval period. A Khond chief called Kulladaha, a feudatory of the Bhanja king Pratapabhanja, was a great devotee of Vyagradevi in the 13th century A.D. Kulladaha roused the wrath of the overlord on account of his unreasonable designs which led to his defeat and exile by the latter. Since then Vyaghradevi became the guardian deity of the Bhanjas of Ghumsar. She was enshrined at the top of a hill at Kullada, which was the capital of the Bhanja kings and now situated at a distance of seven kilometre to the north of Bhanjanagar. At the foot of the hill the Chalanti Pratima (the movable image) of Vyaghradevi is enshrined in a temple constructed by Dhanjaya Bhanja (A.D. 1636-1702).[25] During the reign of Ghana Bhanja (A.D. 1709-1744) human sacrifices were made to propitiate the Goddess.[26] The tribal classes of Ghumasar had a belief that she protected them from tigers and other wild beasts, ascertained fertility and favoured them with good fortune.[27]

The Tara-Tarini temple at the top of a hill, situated on the bank of the river Rishikulya near Purushottampur, which is not far from Jaugada (Samapa) where we find the edicts of Ashoka, is a famous Sakti shrine of Ganjam, even of south Orissa. The shrine is said to have been established by Vasu Praharaja in a tribal surrounding. Two stones anthropomorphised by the addition of silver eyes are the main images of this temple which represent the Goddesses Tara and Tarini. In between them are placed two fully elaborated brass heads as their Chalanti partima. From a tribal cult Tara and Tarini have been transformed into Sakti cult through the process of Aryanization. Of course, the name Tara, the primordial deity of the Mahayana Buddhist pantheon, indicates Buddhist influence or element in the cult of Tara-Tarini which seems to suggest the incorporation of a tribal cult into Buddhism before its Aryanization. That the Tara-Tarini cult is of autochthonous origin is evident from the facts that at Dasahara festival and on every Tuesday of the month of Chaitra animals are sacrificed in front of the temple over a raised platform and their blood is offered to the Goddesses from the raised platform. Secondly the priests of the temple are not Brahmins. Before the British occupation human sacrifices were made to propitiate the Goddesses.

It is interesting to note that one of the legends connects the Tara-Tarini temple with the Brahmanical tradition by regarding it as one of the Sakta Peethas which originated from the limbs of the corpse of Devi or Sati. It is said that once Daksha Prajapati, the father of Parvati, performed a Yajna to which he did not invite Siva or parvati. Thus being insulted Parvati plunged herself into the fire pit of the Yajna and died. Siva immediately rushed to the spot, removed the dead body of Parvati and carried her corpse with him to whichever place he went, as he could not separate himself from her body. Brahma, Vishnu and Sani entered into the corpse by Yoga and disposed of it part by part. Consequently Sakta Peethas originated from the places where the portions (limbs) of Parvati's corpse had fallen. At Tara-Tareni her breasts fell and thus a Sakta Peetha arose at this place.[28].

Another legend says that once upon a time Goddess Durga appeared in the form of two beautiful girls and lived as daughters in the house of Vasu Praharaja, a Tantric scholar of village Vira Jagannathapur Sasana of Athagada in the Ganjam district. After they disappeared all of a sudden, Vasu Praharaja, their foster father, made a thorough search of them, but in vain. However, he saw them in a dream and came to know that they have installed themselves as deities on the top of a nearby hill (the present Tara-Tarini hill). He was directed to worship them. Accordingly, he made all arrangements for their worship on the top of the hill where he found the images. Since then two stones are worshipped by the names Tara and Tarini who are known among the local people as two sisters. The priests of the shrine are the descendants of Vasu Praharaja. Eschmann says "this legend in its present form is no more very elucidating. However, its main elements are clear, the Goddess appears through a human being in a low class or even tribal surrounding. It is her order to be worshipped in surroundings by low caste people through a uniconical symbol. Her sudden disappearance may originally have referred to a sacrifice".[29]

At Kankia on the Kerandimala hill, a spur of the eastern ghats, is the famous shrine of the Goddess Mahuri Kalua, the family deity of the Mahuri Raj family since the 18th century. The shrine is in a tribal environment. Its priests are of tribal origin. Animal sacrifices are offered to the Goddess almost every day to fulfil a desire. In the months of Chaitra and Asvina festivals are held here attended largely by the surrounding hill tribes.

The Budhi Thakurani, the presiding deity of Berhampur town is an aboriginal goddess incorporated into Hinduism. She is considered to be the daughter of the weaver's (Desraj) family who are called the Deras (Devangam in Telugu). They are of the Lingayat sect of non-Aryan origin. The festival of Budhi Thakurani is called the Thakurani Yatra, observed once in two years in the month of Chaitra. It is considered to be a family festival of the Deras, organised by their family head, the Desi Behera. During the festival, which is attended by all sects, the Goddess goes to her Father's house in Desi Behera street from her abode in old Berhampur. A thatched house is erected in front of the house of the Desi Behera for her sojourn during the festival. Tribal dances are a special feature of this festival. The priests of this Goddess are of Sudra origin. Goats, sheep and cocks are sacrificed before the Goddess. All these features suggest that the Budhi Thakurani has been transformed from a tribal cult into Sakti cult under the process of Aryanization.

These aboriginal Goddesses which have been Aryanized were acknowledged as members of the documented theology of the society in whose contact the tribes lived. Thus these Goddesses who are an excellent example for such an acknowledgement as well as for the link between Aryanization and local tradition, have played a prominent role in the folk lore and the cultural heritage of Ganjam.

REFERENCES

1. *Mahabharata, Santi Parva,* LXV (translated by Roy, VIII, p. 146) and by Kulke, Chapter, VII. The Cult of Jagannatha and the Regional Tradition of Orissa, p. 128, 1978.

2. R.S. Sharma, Indian Feudalism, c. 300-1200, p. 281, Calcutta, 1965.
3. D.D. Kosambi, Myth and Reality, p. 85.
4. R.S. Sharma, Material Milieu of Tantrism, Kosambi Memorial Volume, p. 131; B.N.S. Yadav, Problems of Inter-action between Socio-Economic Classes in the Early Medieval Complex, J.H.R. III. i.p. 44; N.N. Bhattacharya, India Mother Goddess, pp. 57-59.
5. D.D. Kosambi, op. cit., p. 90. D.C. Sircar, Sakta Pithas, published from J.R.A.S.B. Letter; Vol. XIV. pp. 12-26 (1949) by Motilal Banarasi Das.
6. N.N. Bhattacharya, op. cit., p. 58.
7. *Varanga Charita*, Chapter 13, verse 58.
8. R.N. Nandi, Religious Institutions and Cults in the Deccan, p. 143, Delhi, 1973.
9. F.E. Pargiter, Ancient Indian Historical Tradition, p. 3.
10. R.N. Nandi, op. cit., p. 120.
11. T.J. Maltby, the Ganjam District Manual, pp. 61-67.
12. Edited by S.N. Rajguru, K.J.H.R.S., Vol. II. No. II, pp. 107-110ff; Re-edited by D.C. Sarcar, E.I., Vol. XXX, pp. 274-8 ff.
13. Inscriptions of Orissa, Vol. I, Part II, p. 84.
14. The Sulkis have attributed every bit of their success and prosperity to the face of the Goddess by the phrase—'Stambhesvari Labdha Vara Prasadat'—vide, J.B.O.R.S., Vol. II, Part IV, December, 1916, pp. 401-3; E.I., Vol. XXVIII, p. 112; J.A.S.B., Vol. LXIV, p. 127; J.B.O.R.S. Vol. IV, Part-II (June, 1918), pp. 168-171; Sudhakara Patnaik, *Kodalaka Mandala Of Stambhesvari* (Oriya article), Utkala Sahitya, now defunct Oriya monthly, Vol. 26, Nos. 3 & 4, pp. 7-15, 1922.
15. Vide Taspaikera charter of Ranaka Rana Bhanjadeva, J.B.O.R.S., Vol. VI, p. 482; J.A.S. 'Bengal' New Series, Vol. VII, No. VII, pp. 443-447 (July 1911); I.H.O., Vol, XXVIII, Part III(1952), pp. 225 ff.
16. Edited by K.C. Panigrahi, Journal of Orissa History, Vol. I, No. I, pp. 1—7, January 1980.
17. T.C. Rath, Asika (Article in Oriya), *Utkala Sahitya*, Vol. XXI, Part—III (1918), p. 136.
18. J.R.A.S.B. Letters, Vol. XIV, p. 104 (1948).

19. R.C. Majumdar, History of Bengal, Dacca University, Vol. I, p. 452, Plate VI; Annual Report, Archaeological Survey of India, 1924—25, p. 155, Plate XLC; N.K. Bhattasali, Iconography of the Buddhist and Brahmanical sculptures of the Deccan Museum, pp. 122-124, Plate LXIV.
20. B.C. Majumdar, Orissa in the Making, p. 107 ff.
21. A. Eschmann, Kulke and Tripathy, The Cult of Jagannatha and the regional tradition of Orissa, Ch. V. p. 93.
22. *Odisara Deva Devi* (book in Oriya), Part II, pp. 122-128.
23. A. Eschmann, Kulke and Tripathy, op. cit, p. 93.
24. K.C. Mishra, The Cult of Jagannatha, p. 15, 1971.
25. Chintamani Mahanty, *Ghumusara Kavya* (in Oriya), p. 51, Cuttack, 1938.
26. T.C. Rath, History of Ghumsar, Cuttack, 1913; *Odisara Deva Devi*, Part II, pp. 23-24, published on behalf of *Utkal Pathaka Samiti.*
27. Macpherson, K. 'Account of Religious Opinion and Observances of the Khonds of Ghumsar and Boud' with lists of deities, J.R.A.S., Vol. II, p. 171 ff.
28. D.C. Sircar, The Sakta Pithas, Delhi (reprint), 1973, p. 6 f and p. 3.
29. A. Eschmann, Kulke and Tripathy, op. cit., p. 92.

3

CHANGING PATTERN OF TRIBAL RELIGIOUS SYSTEM IN ANCIENT ORISSA

Dr. L.K. Panda*

The tribals of Orissa constitute a large section of the population of the State. Their population is roughly twenty five per cent of the total population of Orissa. Of the sixty two Orissan tribes on record, the number of main tribal groups is about a score and a half. Though at present Orissa contains a very large and varied tribal population made up of the Bhuyias, Binjhals, Bhumijas, Gonds, Hos, Juangas, Kharias, Khonds, Koras, Oraons, Santalas, Mundas, Koyas, Bondas, Godabas, Parojas and Sauras or Savaras,[1] only the Savaras and Gonds figure in the epigraphic records. Each tribe has its own peculiar religious customs, dress, social organization and language either inherited or acquired through interaction of many cultural cross-currents, that made inroads into the predominantly forest-covered part of Orissa. Not only that but also the closer association with different later tribal settlers and powerful non-tribal societies has caused mutual adoption of habits and customs either fully or through restraints. In the light of this, we are to study the changing pattern of tribal religious system in ancient Orissa.

*Reader in History, Dhenkanal College, Dhenkanal.

Orissa is located on the gateway of the Northern and the Southern India and as such it is the meeting-ground of the Aryans and the non-Aryans whose religious faith greatly influenced the society and culture of the tribal population of Orissa. Geographical factors mainly contributed to the evolution of the socio-religious life of Orissa from very early times. Being a hilly country its earliest inhabitants were people of the tribal stock. The Pulindas, and the Savaras, in different parts of Orissa, were beyond the pale of Aryan civilization in the protohistoric period. But in the course of the Aryanization, Brahmanical form of Hinduism deeply influenced their life and thought.

Among the various factors which contributed to the evolution of religious life in ancient Orissa, primitive tree worship of the aboriginals formed an important aspect. The native hill tribes of Orissa in course of time came gradually in contact with the Aryans. As a result of this there was an assimilation of the Aryan and the aboriginal culture. The interaction of the two forces led to a synthesis of religious belief which, characterised the growth and development of various religious faiths viz., Saivism. Vaishnavism and Saktism in Orissa through centuries.

Prior to the influx of Brahmanical thoughts and concepts to the heart of Kalinga the aboriginal tribes of Orissa worshipped originally a number of aboriginal deities. The latter invaders who had settled amidst the tribes, in course of time, adopted and worshipped these deities in order to enjoy the confidence and seek the cooperation of the tribals in their settlements. Gradually these deities were Hinduised or Aryanized being transformed from formidable nomadic cult into various Brahmanic cults and worshipped both by the Aryans and the non-Aryan sections of the society. This process of transformation was made by the invaders who, in the meantime, split up themselves into several ruling dynasties and ruled over the tribals, having established kingdoms of their own. Therefore to keep up the tribals in good humour they Aryanized, worshipped and patronised their gods and goddesses and accepted their religious beliefs and concepts. Thus the Hindu religion became a blending of heterogeneous cults embodying the precepts of different tribes in different times.

Mahendragiri in the southern part of Orissa which was a stronghold of the pulindas and the Savaras, was now recognised as a Kulagiri [3] in the Puranas. The Pulindas were also struggling hard for Hinduised social promotion. They believed in the worship of tree which is a pre-Aryan concept. The Savaras who were originally worshippers of tree, became worshippers of Siva-linga whom they adored as 'Sthanu'[4] or 'branchless trunk'. An anecdote of the Skanda Purana [5] indicates as to how the worship of Siva-linga emerged out of tree worship which was the faith of the aboriginal people of Kalinga. This anecdote as recorded in the puranic-lore is widely prevalent among the tribal people of ancient Kalinga. The tribal people used to worship the tree but under the influence of the Brahmanical school, the Sailodbhavas called him 'Sthanu' which means a branchless trunk as well as Lord Siva. The Pulindas and the Savaras, who were the traditional worshippers of Siva, seemed to have been gradually Aryanized under the influence of the Brahmanical school and absorbed the vedic concepts in their socio-religious system. In this process in Orissa the tree worship of the Savaras got itself mingled and merged in the vedic worship of Rudra. Under the influence of the Saivite teachers of the Mattamayura school the pulindas and the Sailajas[6] who emerged as the Sailodbhavas became devout worshippers of Uma-Mahesvara in course of time. This tree-worship prevalent among the aboriginal tribes of Orissa was also synthesised in the Purusottama cult, which was later recognised as Vaishnavism. Purusottama-Jagannath who is worshipped at Puri as Vishnu and Krshna is an image made out of a log of wood (Daru). The deities which are made of log give an indication that they might have been aboriginal in origin In southern Orissa, particularly among the Savaras inhabitating the Mahendragiri region, the deities are made of wood. Jagannath whose other name is Darubrahma might have been a Savara deity. Even today the Savaras worship a log of wood whom they adored as Jaganta or Jagannalo.[7] The resemblance of the names Jagannath and Jaganta and the log of wood was the common medium of worship for both the deities very well indicates the significance of the tree-worship as a common religious practice among the aboriginals, which was subsequently mingled in the Purusottama cult of the Aryans. The legendary association of the Savaras with Nilamadhava, the predecessor of Purusottama-Jagannatha, as described in the Skanda Purana[8] lends support to this presumption. According to a tradition, the images originally enshrined in the temple of Purusottama at Puri were worshipped by Savaras in the hill tracts of Orissa. It is also believed that a section of the *Sevayatas* or the servants of the temple of Purusottama originated from the Savaras. Moreover, the Sirpur stone Inscription of Vasata refers to Nrusimha, an incarnation of Vishnu, as Purusottama who emerged out of a 'stambha' or pillar. The Sailodbhavas who originated from the tribal stock of the Pulindas and the Sailajas, like the Savara visvavasu of the Skanda Purana, popularised the cult of Madhava in Orissa, which was considered part and parcel of Vaishnava worship in the state. These are the basic reference to indicate how the primitive tree-worship of the aboriginals was merged in course of time with the cult of Purusottama-Vishnu in Orissa and how the tribal religious practices were adopted by the Hindus.

Saktism in Orissa also incorporated the tree-worship of the hill tribes into its fold. Stambhesvari, the goddess of the post or pillar, was originally an aboriginal goddess worshipped by the non-Aryan tribes of 'hinterland' Orissa. In course of time she, like many other tribal deities, was given a place in the Hindu pantheon. She was adopted and worshipped by the Aryan invaders who had settled amidst the non-Aryan tribes.[8] Under the influence of the Brahmmnical school, the aboriginals identified the 'Stambha' with the Mother goddess. The hill tribes who believed in matriarchy were worshippers of Sakti.[9] As a result of the fusion of the vedic concept of Uma with the cult of 'Stambha' there emerged the worship of Stambhesvari at least in tribal surroundings. She is the best example of the aboriginal goddess of Orissa which underwent the process of Aryanization in earlier times. The earliest reference to this is found in the Terasinga copper plates[10] of Tustikara, palaeographically assigned to the 4th or the 5th century A.D. who has styled himself as "Stambhesvari Padabhakta". In course of time this cult became popular among some ruling families of the early medieval period in Orissa. The Bhanjas of Khinjalimandala[11] and the Sulkis of Kodalakamandala[12] have recorded in their charters that they achieved success and prosperity through the grace of Stambhesvari, the mother goddess. The Somavamsis were also influenced by this cult. As revealed from the Muranjamura charter [13] Panchambari Bhadrambika was the tutelary deity of the Somavamsis. They indentified this deity Bhadrambika with Stambhesvari when they came in touch with the worship of the log of wood as Stambhesvari. It is most probably this fusion of the cult of Stambhesvari and Bhadrambika which contributed to the evolution of Subhadra,[14] the central wooden figure in the Jagannath triad.

The tribals of Orissa worship the Sun in their own ways either as the supreme being or as a powerful God regulating their agriculture. The changes of weather, the day-breaks and the night falls, and the germination, growth and decay of plants and their effect on human beings led the tribal mind to the worship of this god. Moreover, they invoke this deity to protect their fields, to help them hunt in the wilds, to relieve them of the debts and other unpleasant aspects of life. This is the cause of the tribal cenception about this aspect of nature as the Dharma or the Supreme power. This Sun-worship has been reflected in Mahima Dharma resulting in an important religious sect of Orissa. So it is not strange to find that Bhima Bhoi, the blind poet of the Khonds, as the exponent of this religious cult having largest following in the tribal and other underdeveloped groups of Orissa. Gradually the caste Hindus incorporated this system into the Hindu fold. Hence the sun worship in caste societies is observed on the day of the Samba Dasami or the tenth day of Pausa month. Sun image worship is also witnessed in the Ashramas of caste Hindu societies of Orissa, particularly at Kasyapa-Shrama of the Baujang Village of Badachana police station at Cuttack district.

Thus the aforesaid analysis and interpretation of the source materials lead us to conclude that the Primitive tribal religious system like the tree-worship and the worship of the sun was gradually synthesised into the Hindu religion through different process of interaction and adoption. The Aryan kings or the invaders were mostly dependent upon the support and loyalty of the sturdy tribals. Therefore, they kept them in good humour through gradual process of inclusion of the tribal groups into the Hindu caste system and the absorption and adoption of some aspects of the tribal religion and culture into the Aryan fold. Pargiter, therefore observes[15] that "the Aryans met with the religious practices and beliefs among whom (the tribes) they ruled over or came into lasting contact with and have assimilated some of them gradually thus modifying their own religion to certain extent". In this process the dominant tribal deities were Aryanized and patronised by kings as their tutelary deities enabled the kings to consolidate their power and its legitimation in the Hindu tribal zone of the hilly hinterland of Orissa.[16]

In this process of the Aryanisation, the Brahmanas played an important role. They settled in the forest tracts through land grants and came into contact with the forest tribes which resided in the dominion of the Aryan kings.[17] The Brahmanas codified and defined the duties of the tribes which were to lead a recluse living in the forest and serve their king in various ways.[18] R.S.Sharma has rightly stated that "the significance of land grants to Brahmanas is no difficult to appreciate. The grantees brought new knowledge which improved cultivation and inculcated in the aborigines a sense of loyalty to the established order upheld by the rulers".[19] The co-existence of Brahmanical and tribal cultures led to the interaction between these two.[20] In this way the deities like Siva-linga, Nilamadhava, Stambhesvari and the process of Sun worship, worshipped by the non-Aryan tribes, entered the

Brahmanical pantheon and they are the best examples of gods and goddesses of ancient Orissa which underwent the process of Aryanization in earlier times.

REFERENCES

1. Banerjee, R.D. History of Orissa, I, p. 19
2. Sircar, D.C. Select Inscription, I, (Calcutta, 1965), p. 100.
3. Vamana Purana, Canto XIII, Vr. 14.
4. I.O.I., pt. II, p. 167, Apte, V. Students' Sanskrit Dictionary (Delhi, 1963), p. 622.
5. Rajguru, S.N. Invocatory Verses from the Inscriptions Vol. II, pp.V-VI.
6. Behera, S.C. Rise and Fall of the Sailodbhavas, (Calcutta, 1982), pp.171-174.
7. Das, M.N. (ed.) Sidelights in the History and Culture of Orissa (Cuttack, 1977), p. 380.
8. Skanda Purana, (Vishnu Khanda), Ch. VII, Vr. 97. Mazumdar, B.C. Orissa in the Making, p.107, J.A.S.B. New Series, Vii. (1911) pp. 443-47.
9. Bhattacharya, N.N. India Mother Goddesses, pp. 57-59, Kosambi, D.D. Myth and Reality, p.85.
10. J.K.H.R.S.,Vol. II, No.2, pp,107-110, E.I. XXX, pp. 274-278.
11. I.O., VI, p.67.
12. "Stambhesvari Labdha Vara Prasadah"—J.B.O.R.S,, II pt. IV (December, 1916), pp. 400-405.
13. I.O. VI, p. 219
14. Ray, B.C. (Ed.) Culture: Heritage of Orissa, Vol.I, p. 5.
15. Pargiter, F.E., Ancient Indian Historical Tradition, p.3.
16. Eschmann, Kulke and Tripathi, The Cult of Jagannath and the Regional Traditions of Orissa (1978). pp. 128-129.
17. Kosambi, D.D., Myth & Reality, p. 91.
18. The Mahabharata, Santi Parva (Translated by Roy, VIII, pp. 1-6).
19. Sharma, R.S. Indian Feudalism c.300-1200, p.28, (Calcutta, 1965).
20. Yadav, B.N.S., I.H.R., III, pt. i, p.44.

4

SOCIO-CULTURAL CHANGES OF TRIBAL LIFE UNDER THE BRITISH RULE IN ORISSA

M.M. Mohapatra*

The British administrative policy in respect of the conquered Indian territories had two main strands—one towards the vast general public of the plain areas and another towards the tribal people of the mountainous regions and it was the latter that merited the urgent and favourable attention of the British administrators in view of its utter backwardness. The entire gamut of socio-cultural life of the tribals that came under the purview of British administration has now become a subject of study by anthropologists, sociologists and of late by historians too. The matter is of vital interest more particularly to the historians as the changes effected by the various British administrative measures are far-reaching and multi-dimensional from the tribal point of view.

That no aboriginal tribe has been so much influenced between 1855-97 by an alien admin'stration as were the Khonds of Baud Maliahs, a tribal tract under Bengal Presidency is evident from the following observations. Although basically a hill race and intensely averse to absorb any alien

* Lecturer in History, Khallikote College, Berhampur.

culture, yet, the native inhabitants of Khondmals could not remain isolated from the civilizing mission of their new masters, the British.

During the British rule a new class was created known as the Mutha head or Mutha Sardar of Mallik from among the Khond Community whose social status was gradually recognized by the latter. These village leaders who helped the British administration in tax collection and police functions served as a vital link between the administrators and the governed and these offices became, in due course of time, hereditary.[2] By suppressing inhumane practices like meriah sacrifice, witchcraft and such other superstitious beliefs widely prevalent among the Khonds, the British have helped raise the Khond Community to a higher plane of civilized world.[3]

In the initial stage of existence, the Khonds had a self-sustained economy. They were an easy-going nomadic tribe living primarily on hunting and jungle products. In due course of time, these aborigines resorted to shifting cultivation which, to some extent, supplemented their means of subsistence. Yet, a majority of them could save very little and had to starve during a stated period of every year. Noticing this plight of the Khonds, the British authorities had taken sufficient precautionary measures like hoarding of food-grains in godowns, advancing loans for the purchase of agricultural tools and implements and providing marketing facilities for the sale of their agricultural products at a reasonable price. The local administration was also alert to save the credulous and needy Khonds from economic exploitation at the hands of rapacious and unscrupulous traders of the plain areas.[4]

A semi-military security force was raised from among the hill-men, recruits being mostly paiks, the landed militia.[5] Demand for labourers for the construction of roads, forest guard and teachers in school in the tribal areas brought into being a class of men, economically dependent on the British Government and serving as purveyors of new influences on the tribal people. British Administration brought in its wake a change in the concept of land ownership. Contrary to tradition, membership of a clan was no longer the only title to land nor could new lands be acquired by arms. Now the Government was the new source of power and it guaranteed property as the surest means of maintaining peace among the Khonds which the latter regarded as a sense of benefit from contact with the British rule.[6]

The Khond's exposure to an alien administration like that of the British, helped contribute both to the improvement and degradation of their economic status. Their economic frontier continued to expand in proportion to changes in the social frontier.[5] Their sources of income tended to get more diversified. They served as labourers to make roads. Some of them became in course of time small traders, some of them served as watchmen in Government rest houses, some came down to the plains for their livelihood. The inevitable replacements of the barter economy by money economy was indeed a great economic change. It also facilitated easier communication between the tribals and the people of plains.[7]

With the opening up of roads and the more frequent relations with the plainsmen as traders and agents of the Government new tastes and new wants were noticed growing among the Khonds. They now used articles imported from the plains such as soap, fine cloth, tea, hair oil and cigarettes. The Khond habits tended to change when at fairs and markets set up by the Government, they could get things for which earlier they had to depend on the Panos. The tribesmen could now get far greater value for their wares for sale besides meeting their own wants more cheaply than before. Visits of Government officers gave some impetus to local trade of the hill Khonds. The tribesmen gradually overcame their fear of the British, they trekked several miles to reach Government Officers' camps to sell their local products and to procure beads, mirrors and red cloth from the officers.[8] Mr. T.E. Ravenshaw, the then Commissioner for Orissa Divi-noticing the changing socio-economic life of the Khond tracts sion, reported to the Government as follows. "The Khonds formerly possessed little property of any sort. A red cloth or a brass plate was rare. Nowadays in most of the more respectable houses one sees brass vessels in tolerable profusion. They have acquired considerable wealth in silver and brass ornaments; and where they formerly went half-starved and half-naked, they have now abundance of food and a liberal supply of raiment. Cultivation is extended and they grow large quantity of cotton, oil seeds and turmeric for export.[9]"

Although the British had recognized on principle the utility of spreading education among the tribals in general as one of the surest means of bringing them to the door-steps of civilization yet they had to lower the tempo of such civilizing zeal as they encountered the major hurdle of apathy from the aborigines themselves. The tribal population of the Khondmals could not cope up with the tremendous vigour and zeal with which their alien administrators endeavoured to educate them. The more the rulers exhibited their interest to make education popular among the tribals with the declared intention of protecting them from exploitation, the more the latter became suspicious and fearful about the Government's motive. However the Government went ahead with its programme and set up a few number of schools as the first step of its mission. Khond students could be brought on rolls in the school attendance register after much persuasion. Even promises and tempting rewards were held out to achieve the purpose. In the initial stage, the attendance was very low but subsequently it showed an upward trend of substantial increase.

As regards the Khond people and their education, there was much truth in the remark of Mr. Lloyd, Tehsildar of Khondmals from May 1892 to Aug' 1894 that the Khonds required teachers of their own clan and caste, a want which was not difficult on the part of the Government to overcome by the endeavour of the local officers in utilizing the services of the few Khond students turned out every year by the primary schools in the sub-division.[10]

The British officers were also keen to adopt such measures which would to help protect the Khond subjects from economic ruination. Like many other tribals the Khonds were addicted to liquor brewed at their homes, out of mahua flower. Local sundhis and some other persons were usually engaged in distilling wine and carrying on illicit sale of liquor. Very stringent measures were taken by the British authorities prohibiting its profuse use in the area, otherwise indiscriminate sale of liquor would have further deteriorated the economic condition of the people. Most often the Khonds used to mortgage their best lands for the sake of indulging in the pleasure of intoxication. Taking advantage of this weakness among the Khonds, the Oriya interlopers amassed huge fortunes by fraud, deceit and chicanery.[11]

With a view to keeping the outsiders, as far as practicable, out of the Khondmals, the Government proposed to assess them heavily. Transfers of lands were unrecognized by the court between Khonds and others. This was the expedient by which the British authorities thought it possible to protect the Khonds in the possession of the Mals from ultimate extinction. The Government also took another drastic measure to prevent the absorption of cultivable tracts by 'outsiders' to such an extent as shall not allow the Khonds some room for the extension of cultivation.[12]

A great cause of alienation of lands disappeared with the decrease of the number of outsiders in Khondmals from 400 to about 20 only. Another proposal of a somewhat drastic nature to prevent alienation of lands in the Khondmals in future also received immediate consideration of the Bengal Government and as a result of which no outsiders were permitted to take up lands within Khondmals without the consent of the Khond Mallicks or headmen and village headmen ordered not to allow any new settlers other than the Khonds within their village boarders until the matter has been reported to and sanctioned by the S.D.O. who would have to register all sanctioned settlers and their holdings. Thus registration of mortgage and sale deeds became statutory in the Khondmals sub-division of Angul District.[13] With regard to the administration of justice, the British had to become still more cautious in their approach. They did not like to put into effect the English laws in the Khondmals until the Khonds had attained a level to comprehend its implications. In the early years of their administration, the British authorities tried their best to impress upon the wild tribes of Khondistan that they were sincere and honest in their pledges to serve the ends of justice. Initially, the Khonds had no inclination to bring their cases to the doors of English law courts but in due course they exhibited more eagerneess to seek relief in the courts than to have recourse to their village panchayats whose judgements were, at times, more partial and severe.[14]

Thus the conclusion that may be drawn from the foregone analysis is that the British administrative policy had affected the socio-cultural life of this important section of the tribal people of Orissa under review to an extent that did not result in the total annihilation of the cultural identity of the latter. In a way the process of change was slow and steady and it was effected more through persuasion than through intimidation and coercion. Both the sides have shown a remarkable sense of understanding for each other's point of view. The spirit of accommodation from the Government and that of assimilation from the governed has made the process of change smooth and the effect lasting.

REFERENCES

1. C.H. Marindin, Superintendent of Tributary Mahals, Orissa, No. 1262 p. dt. 12fth August, 1899 to the Chief Secretary, Govt. of Bengal.
2. K. Majumdar, Studies in History, XVIII Annual Session, Institute of Historical Studies, Nagpur.
3. J.A. Campbell, A Personal Narrative of Thirteen Years Service Among the Hill Tribes of Hindustan (London, 1864).
4. Man in India Vol. 56, Jan-March 1976 No. 1 page. 52.
5. BJCP, 19 June 1843 No. 105, Home Deptt. Minute, 31 May 1843.
6. F.C. Bailey, Caste and Economic Frontier: A Village in Highland Orissa (Manchester, 1957), P.P. 5,9.

7. Ibid.
8. Govt. of Bengal Political proceedings, July 1863 No. 15.
9. E.T. Dalton, Descriptive Ethnology of Bengal (Indian-Edition, New Delhi, 1974) P. 301.
10. Annual Administration Reports 1893-94 No. 1474 p. dt. 21st July 1894, from H.G. Cooke, Officiating Supdt. Tributary Mahals, Orissa, to the Chief Secretary, Govt. of Bengal.
11. J.C. Lloyd, S.D.O., Khondmals, No. 362 dt. 22nd Feb-1887.
12. Bengal Govt. Resolution No. 825, dt. 20th Sept, 1894.
13. C.W. Bolton, Officiating Chief-Secretary to Govt. of Bengal No. 139 PD dt. 30th June, 1896 to the Secretary, Govt. of India, Foreign Deptt.
14. Annual Administration Reports of the Khondmals from 1855-56 to 1882-83.

5

RELIGIOUS RITES AND FESTIVALS OF THE TRIBES OF ORISSA

Dr. N.K. Behura & K.K. Mishra*

Religion of the tribes of Orissa is different from the mystic religions of advanced societies. Among the tribals the pantheon consists of the supreme Sun God, Mother Earth, presiding deities, nature spirits, ancestral spirits and the village tutelary. Supernatural rites are explicitly directed towards happiness and security in this world, abundance of natural resources and crops, and avoidance of sickness. There is no concept of "Heaven" and "Hell", and reward or punishment for moral and immoral acts during life-time. After death the soul is called back to join the ancestral spirits in the sacred domestic tabernacle. There is belief in reincarnation and transmigration of souls into various forms of life; trees, birds, animals etc. But there is no connection between ethical action and the form of reincarnation. No idol or image and no temple in well-defined form is found, although rudiments of idolatory is there (Sinha, 19).

The natural universe is charged with impersonal and personalized spirits or supernatural powers. Man, nature

*Professor Dept. of Anthropology, Utkal University, Vani Vihar, Bhubaneswar.

and supernatural are connected in terms of infinite relationship.

In Orissa there are 62 Scheduled Tribes, who are at different levels of socio-economic development, and belong to three linguistic families. On the basis of economic pursuit Orissa tribes can be divided into three categories: (i) Gatherer-hunters, (ii) Gatherer-shifting cultivators, and (iii) Gatherer-settled agriculturists. Mankidia and Hill-Kharia belong to the first category; Juang, Pauri-Bhuyan, Khond, Savra, Didayaee, Jharia, Pengo, Koya and Bonda are in the second category; and the Santals, Ho, Munda, Bathudi, Bhumij, Oraon, Kisan, and Gadaba are in the third category.

The religion of Orissa tribes is an admixture of life-crisis rites, cyclic group rites, ancestral and totemic rites, observance of taboos and practice of occultism in various forms.

Crisis Rites

Outstanding among crisis rites are those connected with the important, critical, but normally expectable events in the life, birth, sexual maturity, marriage and death. Rituals performed on these occasions have been called rites of passage because they involve transition from one social status to another. Crisis rituals include three- phased observances which signify separation of individuals from one particular social status, transition from one social status to another, and integration into a higher social status. Crisis rites are markers of special events in the life of the individual and are different from recurrent cyclic rituals pertaining to sowing and harvesting. Happenings such as birth, sexual maturity, marriage, illness or death are extremely important to an individual and his close relatives, and are generally of diminishing importance outside his kinship circle. Another distinction between crisis rites and cyclic rites is that the first may involve gain or loss of social members, but in the second no change of personnel is implied.

Crisis rituals are important in all societies. They signify

movement from one status to another and loss or gain of societal members. Arnold Van Gennep, who coined the expression "rites of passage", saw these rites as means by which individuals are eased through the difficulties of transition from one social role to another. He contended that all these rituals are divided into three consecutive elements called in French, separation, marge, and aggregation, which are translated as separation, transition and reintegration. For instance, in the rite of sexual maturity an individual is first severed from his old status, than remains in a period of transition, and finally is reintegrated into the new status. These three stages are clearly seen in the ritual observances among the tribes of Orissa.

Birth Rite

Birth is an important bio-social event in every society. While bringing out change in the status of married couple it increases the number of societal members. It causes fresh alignment in structural relations. It often causes a sharp break with the conventions of the past. The parents and the child upon whom the birth rite centres are separated physically and socially from other members of society for varying periods. The period of segregation is the period of ritual pollution, which indeed is the transition period. The duration of the transition period varies from tribe to tribe. The persons, on whom this ritual hinges, observe certain taboos and refrain from sacred activities. Among the Hinduised tribes Gond, Savar, Deshia Khond, Rajkuli Bhuyan, Bhumij, Bathudi etc. simulation of the Brahmanical concepts of purity and pollution are found to a considerable extent. Temporarily segregated persons are reintegrated into their society after the birth rite, and the newly born child is also admitted to the society of its parents. Name-giving ceremony mostly goes along with this rite.

Pubescent Rite

Among the tribal people of Orissa sexual maturity of boys is not punctuated by any rite. Simply a young man's sexual maturity is recognized on the basis of the change in his voice, and on eruption of mustache, beard and armpit hairs. But the maturity of a girl, on the other hand, is a very significant personal and social event, because it is the woman who bears children. Attainment of puberty by a girl immediately leads to her physical and social segregation. This abruptly snaps her girlhood, and the menstrual flow is considered a danger. For seven days the girl is kept in strict seclusion and is subjected to observance of taboos. On the expiry of the period of segregation she undergoes a purificatory ritual. Through the ritual the event is announced not only among the kins, but also among neighbours and others of the society. Sexual maturity marks the transition from childhood to adolescent status, a time of marked change in social relations. Among all the tribes of Orissa familiar stages of rites of passage are clear, i.e., isolation and restrictions on behaviour, a period of transition for adjustment, and finally, formal social recognition of transition to the status of adulthood. Use of certain additional forms of ornamentation, including distinctive clothing and hair-dress signify attainment of adulthood. The social importance of these insignia is seriously valued among all the tribes. Physical maturity is dangerous and socially disruptive as it often causes remarkable change in the behaviour of an individual.

Marriage Rite

Marriage is a remarkable event in the life of every individual, whether primitive of advanced. Marriage rite is an elaborate one which begins with the attempts for bride acquisition to her affiliation with her affinal kingroup and sexual consummation. Although the rules of residence after marriage and customs of tracing descent are uniform among the tribes of Orissa, other factors, such as mode of acquisition of a bride, payment of bride-price, and age at marriage vary widely among them. Marriages may fall as under, although most marriages are stable, but important is the degree of sacralization attached to marriage institution in all the tribal societies. It is vital to the social identification of children and the continuation of lineages, clans, and other functioning social groups. Marriage rite among the tribes of Orissa not only confers exclusive sexual right on a couple, but cements the social bond between kins of the husband and wife. Most marriages are stable, because a divorce may mean forfeiture or return of bride-price as per customary laws. Marriage in tribal societies is governed by strong social sanction, hence all forms of conjugal unions are legitimized by follow up marriage ceremonies. Among all the tribes of Orissa, especially in respect of marriage by capture, marriage by intrusion and marriage by elopement, the marriage ritual is a post factum event. Social recognition is accorded to the union only when this ritual is gone through, and it takes place when all problems relating to the union are sorted out.

In the past, among all the tribes marriage ritual for men used to be more elaborate than women. But as the advanced sections among them are steadily changing over to negotiated marriages, due importance is also given to girls' marriages.

Marriage brings about significant alterations in the behaviour of both men and women. In a patrilineal society on marriage a woman is separated from her natal kingroup and she undergoes a brief period of transition and adjustment before being integrated into her affinal kingroup.

Among the tribes of Orissa marriage ceremonies are simplest of all rites connected with the events in the life cycle of the individual.

Funeral Rite

Classic features of rites of crisis are often most clearly evident in obsequies. The bereaved refrain from many normal acts: they perform various rites of mourning for the prescribed period which varies from tribe to tribe and finally the funeral or mortuary rite is performed, which marks the end of final formal mourning and after this the kins of the deceased are brought back to normal social relationships.

The degree of elaboration of the funeral rite depends upon the social position of the deceased. The socio-cultural dimension of the rite is directly related to the age and social position of the deceased. In the obsequies of an infant neither more persons are involved nor more resources are spent, as it is considered not a full-fledged member of its society. On the other hand the death of an adult, say the headman or the priest has an important bearing on the lives of many persons and becomes a suitable occasion for larger participation and elaboration of the funeral rite. As all the tribes of Orissa are patrilineal, funeral rites for males are more elaborate than those which are for females.

Ethnographic facts attest that among the tribes of Orissa, both Mundari and Dravidian ones, two funeral rites are conducted. For instance, among the Santals the preliminary purification is called 'telnahan' and the final purification is called 'Bhandan'. The preliminary or green funeral rite is performed shortly after death; and the final or dry funeral rite is held at an interval of a year or so.

The general belief is that the souls of the deceased do not leave their home environment until the final funeral rite is over. "A widow continues to be her deceased husband's wife until this second ceremony, and if she becomes pregnant in the interval between funerals, the child is his and shares in his property" (Norbeck, 1961:160).

In the final funeral rite relatives, and kins of the deceased participate intensively. Men take active parts, and women, whose ritual status is lower, assist them. Mourning roles of the close relatives of the deceased vary according to their relationship to the deceased.

Death permanently separates a person from his family, kins and society, which necessitates fresh adjustment in social relations. The soul of the deceased enters a period of adjustment or transition as much as the bereaved members. The final funeral rite removes pollution incurred by death and restores everyone to a condition of purity and of proper relations within the society as well as with the supernatural world. Funeral rite does not assuage grief, rather it is a means of meeting grief and restoring order which was affected by death.

Annual Cycle of Rituals or Cyclical Group Rites

A ritual is a prescribed order for performing a concatenation of rites, and a rite is a traditional performance to which conventional symbolic meaning is attached by those who believe in it. The rituals are commonly but not always ceremonial in nature. A ritual brings human beings into relationship with gods, ancestral spirits or other supernaturals. Rituals indeed make overt any religion and reenact the interrelationship between cosmographical, supernatural and social worlds.

"Fixed, recurrent group rites that have nearly equal significance for all or most members of the social group in which they are preformed range from familial ceremonies to those which apply to whole societies" (Norbeck' 1961:164). The time of observance of these rites is correlated with the rhythmic cyclical changes in nature. Indeed many of these rites follow the annual cycle of seasons and vis-a-vis the position of the sun and moon in the zodiac during a calendar year. Among the tribes of Orissa excepting those that are Hinduised, observance of daily, weekly and monthly rites is almost nil. Most of rituals among them are seasonal and annual.

As most of the tribes of Orissa practise agriculture in some form or the other and as the rest of others have a vital stake in agriculture, sowing, planting, first-fruit eating and harvest rites are common and important. Their common cyclical rites revolve round the pragmatic problem of ensuring a stable economic condition, recuperation of the declining fertility of soil, protection of crops from damage, human and livestock welfare, safety against predatory animals and venomous reptiles and insuring a good yield of annual and perennial crops.

The annual cycle of rite commence from the time of clearing hill slopes during the Hindu month of Chaitra (March-April) among Juang, Bhuyan, Khond, Soura, Gadaba, Jharia, Didayee, Koya, Bonda and others who practise shifting cultivation: and among others it starts in the month of Baisakh (April-May) with the first-furit ceremony of mango. Other group or community rites follow in a cyclical manner. All the rites centering agriculture, first-fruit eating, human, livestock and crop welfare are observed by the members of a village on a common date, jointly determined by the village headman and the priest, as these are of immense importance to the group or community.

Observance of rites among the Orissan tribes directly depend upon the annual cyclical changes in the physical environment. Summer, monsoon, autumn, winter and spring seasons bring in regular periodic changes in the physical environment which cause change in vegetation and economic activities of the tribals. Indeed these are the times, varying in accordance with their interpretation of the universe, when primitive men by means of magical ritual assure themselves of success in agriculture, hunting, fishing and gathering of fruits, nuts, tusser and roots which will follow or seek supernatural aid and offer oblations for it in these enterprises (Norbeck, 1961: 164).

All the cyclical rites of the tribes of Orissa receive society-wide observance, and these are the occasions of common festivities, elaborate revelry, such as putting on new clothings, feasting, gift-exchange, prolonged bouts of drinking and long sessions of dancing. The rites are observed first at the village level and then at domestic level in every household. At the village level the village priest (called Nicke among the Santal, Pahan among Ho and Munda, Jani among Khond. Pusari among the Gond, Disari among the Gadaba, Parma among the Koya, Nagam among the Juang, Dehuri among the Bhuyan etc.) along with the village headman. The village priest propitiates the supreme god, mother earth commonly on all occasions in addition to the concerned departmental or presiding deity of a specific rite. For instance, among the Santals on *Baha* or *Salei Bonga* ritual, which is observed in the month of phagun (February-March), Chand Bonga, Marang Buru and Zaheerera are propitiated as a matter of routine and the *Baha* or *Salei Bonga* is propitiated especially at the village shrine, called *Zaheerathan.* Similarly among the Juangs on the occasion of Ashadhi rite, which is observed in Ashadha (June-July) Dharamdeota and Basukimata are propitiated along with

Gangeshwariya, the deity responsible for resuscitation of the lost fertility of soil, by the Nagam at the *Garamsiri* or village shrine. The Khond too worship Hira Penu and Takrani Penu along with Jatrakudi Penu during *Baisakh* (April-May) at the village Kuddi by the village Jani and Bejuni.

The number of cyclical group rituals vary from tribe to tribe, but they pertain to protection of humans against disease and malevolent spirits, welfare of their livestock, and healthy growth of crops. As they live under harsh physical conditions, they are very particular about the observance of the group rituals, and by fulfilling their ritual obligation they hope that the nature will continue to be benign and bountiful.

There is no symbolism in the rites of the tribes of Orissa, excepting when a *shaman* licks the blood of a sacrifical creature being possessed by a spirit. The normal articles that are offered in a rite include fruits, nuts, vegetables, corns, flowers, twigs and liquor. Besides, the blood of a sacrificial animal or bird, eggs, which are considered euphemistic offerings, are used in domestic rites and not in group rites.

It is needless to repeat here that every tribe has its pantheon, and the deities of the pantheon are propitiated through various group rites. Group or community rites are the occasions of festivities, when they totally suspend all productive manual work and indulge in revelry and merry-making.

The Santal pantheon consists of Chand Bonga, the supreme creator, *Marang Buru*, the chief deity, *Zaheerera, Lita, Maneka*, and *Tureko*. Next come a couple of village Bongas, Sima Bonga, the presiding deity of village boundary, Bahara Bonga, the deity of village, Majhi Bonga, the spiritual counterpart of the founder of the village, *Tandi Bonga* or the *Khut* (sub-clan) deity, the *Haplamko* Bonga, the lineage deity, Abge Bonga, the family tutelary, and *Ata Bonga*, the manes. All these *Bongas* are benevolent.

Besides the benevolent Bonga, there are innumerable malevolent Bongas, such as Kisar Bonga, Naihar Bonga, Jodha

Bonga, Bhagut Bonga, which cause illness, loss of live-stock and damage of crop.

Santal Shrines

In a Santal village normally there are three shrines, namely, the Jaheerathan, situated outside the village settlement, but within the village boundary; the Majhithan, located just in front of the house of the village headman or Majhi; the Jantal-Jaheera, which is the common shrine of a cluster of Santal villages.

Santal Religious Functionaries

The religious functionaries of a Santal village are : the *Nicke*, the *Kndum Nicke*, the *Chukua Nicke*, the Ojha, and the Jánguru. Nicke is the chief village priest, and the position is hereditary; Chukua Nicke is the assistant of the Nicke. There are two such assistants in every village. The post is not hereditary, and one continues in the post so long one is a bachelor. *Ojha* is the shaman and medicine-man, and *Janguru* is the witch-diviner.

Cycle of Santal Festivals

The Santal Calendar begins with the Hindu month of Phagun (February-March) and ends in the month of *Magh* (January-February). Throughout the year Santals observe a number of festivals and rites. Group rites are accompanied by festivities and fanfare. Santals refer to their festivals as *parb* and to the ritual aspect of the *parb* as *bonga*.

In the month of Phagun they celebrate the Salei Bonga or Baha Bonga. The rite is observed at the *Jaheerathan* by the Nicke with the assistance of Chukua Nicke. The festival ushers in the Santal new year with the offering of sal (shorea robusta) flower ritually to the Bongas.

Ero Bonga festival of the Santal is connected with their first sowing of paddy seeds in the month of *Jestha* (May-June). After this festival Santals are free to sow seeds in their own fields. It is the Nicke who performs the ritual at the *Jaheerathan*.

In the month of Ashadha (June-July) Santals observed *Ashadhia Bonga* for the healthy growth of paddy saplings. The ritual is observed at the Jaheerathan by the Nicke. Santals believe that this ritual eliminates weeds and pests from their paddy fields.

Santals observe *Jon-Nawai* festival in the month of Bhadar (August-September) for offering of the first corns to the *Bongas*.

The *Saharae Bonga* festival is celebrated in the month of Saharea or Kartik (October-November), which marks the beginning of their winter harvest. This is a festival of great revelry and rejoice.

They observe the *Magh Bonga* in the month of Magh (January-February) which marks the end of Santal year. After this festival Santals are free to re-thatch or renovate the roof of their houses.

Santal Rites

Among the Santals there are three group rites, namely, *Marang Kulu*, *Tandi Bonga* and *Haplamko Bonga*. The *Marang Kulu* is observed once a year at the outskirts of the village by the Ojha or Shaman on behalf of the whole village for elimination of sickness, disease and calamity from the village. *Tandi Bonga* is observed once a year for the well-being of *Khut* or sub-clan members in the common *Khut* land by the *Khut-Nicke*. Similarly the *Haplamka Bonga* is observed once a year for the well-being of the members of a lineage by the eldest living member of a village at the outskirts of the village, but in the lineage land.

The life-cycle rituals of the Santals comprise *Janam-Chaitar* or birth ritual, *Nartha* or name-giving ceremony, *Bepla* or marriage ritual and obsequies.

Taboos

The concept of taboo is very wide among the tribes of Orissa. It applies equally to sacred and profane.

Shamanism

Shamanism is the realm of the unknown. Some scholars find its origin in hunting cultures, whereas some others see its origin in agrarian cultures. The term shaman in its widest sense refers to a man or woman who serves a society as a part-time religious practitioner. Sometimes, he or she appears to be emotionally somewhat unstable, easily subject to epileptic fits or frenzies and to self-hypnosis. This is the case among the Saura, Koya, Khond, Gadaba, Jharia and other tribes of south Orissa. This is not so among others, for instance, among the Santal, Ho, Munda, Juang and Bhuyan the shaman is not required by his profession to do more than perform routine and somewhat monotonous rituals.

Among the Saora, Koya and Khond, both men and women become shamans, and among the Juang, Santal, Ho and Munda usually men become shamans.

Among the Saora shamans are known as Kuranmaren and shamanins as Kuranboi, among the Khond shamans as Beju and shamanins as Bejuni, among the Koya shaman as Wadda and shamanin as Waddemute, and among Santals shaman as Ojha and diviner as Janguru.

The shaman has very important pseudo religious functions in almost all the tribal societies of Orissa. But the role of shaman is different from that of the priest. A shaman acquires his status through a personal communication from a supernatural spirit, whereas a priest does not necessarily have a face to face relationship with the spirit world but must have competence in conducting rituals. Shaman performs a curing rite for the benefit of one or more patients. Shamanistic rites are non-calendarical or contingent upon occasions of mishap or illness, whereas the priests or the priestly cult conducts ceremonies which is a public rite performed for the benefit of the whole village or community. Such rites are calendarical or are performed at critical points in ecological cycle.

In Koya society shaman is designated as Wedde. The medicine man is referred to as Malte Weddo, the sorcerer as

Kaimul Wadde, and a witch as Elatant. A Melta Wadde is also a diviner ; he discovers the etiology of diseases for all those who suffer from diseases. He helps people in various ways. There are three types of Melta Wadde, namely, Roto, Sira and Paen. The status of the Roto, is the lowest and that of the Paen is the highest; the Sira enjoys an intermediate status.

Among the Khond Shamans are referred to as Beju and shamanins as Bejuni. Each shaman or shamanin has his or her own spirit to whom he or she regularly propitiates and appeases to get help during his or her occult practices. Through rites and spirit possession shamans or shamanins get into trance during which they are believed to visualize and talk to the spirits who can help mitigate the plight, tribulation and suffering of his or her client.

The Santal medicine man, called Ojha, is a sorcerer. He cures diseases of his clients by administering herbal medicines as well as by propitiating spirits or Bongas. Some of the Ojhas also function as witch-doctors and undertake exorcism.

The Ojhas diagnose sickness and sufferings of their clients through divinations. They are considered seers. After deciphering the cause an Ojha exercises the malevolent spirit through shamanistic rites and chanting of forceful occult spells. Ojha is very much respected in Santal society. Shaman occupies an important position in the Santal society.

REFERENCES

Burkharin, N. 1925. Historical Materialism—A System of Sociology.

Durkheim, E. 1915. The Elementary Forms of Religious life.

Evans-Pritchard, E.D. 1965. Theories of Primitive Religion London : Oxford University Press.

Frazer, J.G. 1922. Golden Bough.

Freud, S. 1950. Totem and Taboo, London : Routledge and Kegan Paul.

Mareth, R. R. 1914. T Threshold of Religion.

Norbeck, E. 1961. Religion in Primitive Society, New York : Harper and Row.

Smith, W.R. 1927. The Religion of the Semitic.

Sinha, S. "Tribal Cultures of Peninsular India as a Dimension of Little Tradition in the study of Indian Civilization", American Folklore.

6

ADIVASIS OF MAYURBHANJ : AN ANALYSIS OF CULTURAL GROWTH

Dr. Mohan Lal Sahoo*

Mayurbhanj is the name of a district lying at the northern border of the state of Orissa in the Indian Union. Its east, north and west are bounded by the States of Bengal and Bihar and in the south it is bounded by the district of Balasore of Orissa. It also adjoins a little portion of the district of Keonjhar in the south-west.

The district of Mayurbhanj was formed in 1948 out of the ex-State of Mayurbhanj. The rulers of the Bhanja dynasty continued to rule over this state in unbroken succession since about the 9th century A.D. The name of the state under the early Bhanja rulers was Khichingkot. The copper plate inscription issued by those rulers indicate that Khichingkot was an extensive territory comprising the present Mayurbhanj and Keonjhar districts as well as parts of Singhbum district in Bihar and Midnapur district in West Bengal. During the Mughal period, the territory of Bhanja rulers extended as far as the sea (east side of the Bay of Bengal). In 1751 Mayurbhanj came under the Marathas and it was during the

*Lecturer in Oriya, Banki College, P.O. Banki Dist. Cuttack.

Maratha rule over Mayurbhanj that the state was deprived of many taluks in the east. It also came under British occupation in 1803. During the period 1803 to 1834 the Kols of Bamanghaty rose in rebellion against the state and Jadunath Bhanja, the then Raja of Mayurbhanj handed over four large Kolpirs of Bamanghaty to the British Government. From that time no other territorial loss occurred till the merger of Mayurbhanj with Orissa on the lst January 1949. The district of Mayurbhanj may be divided into three natural divisions--(1) The Eastern, (2) The Western and (3) The Central region.

The eastern division slopes gently from the foot of the hills towards the sea and served by a number of hill-streams, forms an ideal country for irrigation. It has two sub-divisions namely Raptipada and Baripada.

The western part is fully covered with dense sal forest with many rocky mounds, extends from Suliapada, a hilly taluk to the border of West Bengal and Bihar.

The central portion of the district is covered by a group of hills known as Similipal hills. The Maghasani hill which rises to a height of 3,824 feet is situated in the southern extremity of this group.

The district of Mayurbhanj covers 4022 sq. miles with a total population of 158, 1873 according to the Census of 1981. Out of this nearly 58.56% are Scheduled Tribes. A vast area of the district is barren, uncultivated and hilly ; and a considerable part is covered by forest leaving small pockets only here and there for agriculture. Rainfall is scarce, being 40" on an average for the district. Rice, which is the principal crop, is very difficult to grow for want of adequate rainfall. Drought, scarcity of food and famine is chronic over almost the entire area. The district is educationally most backward in Orissa. The people of the soil are generally poor and have a very low standard of living, but they are very vigorous and hard-working even without adequate food. The district apparently is rich in minerals, but proper exploitation of these minerals have not yet been made. At one time, raw lac, tassar and Sabai grass used to be cultivated on a very large scale and contributed to the economic development of the rural area, but this also is now on decline. Mayurbhanj has a very glorious history as old as pre-Christian eras, and the scholars have felt the existence of elements of pre-historic culture in this area. Living aside the specimens of palaeolithic and neo-lithic culture recovered from Mayurbhanj, if we come to the historic age we find that during the 8th and 9th century A.D. Buddhism was preached in this area before Brahmanism came into existence.

The district of Mayurbhanj is extremely important from anthropological point of view. It is inhabited by almost all the important Scheduled Tribes found in the eastern regions of India though it is also a fact that only a few of them have a concentrated settlement here. Of those tribes who have integrated settlement in the district, mention may be made of Santal, the Hos, Bhumijas, the Bhunya, the Bathuri, and the Gond. Other forty groups of tribes are found scattered around the whole district but they are very few in number. There are isolated settlements of caste Hindu also, scattered over the entire district; but, they are all migrants from outside, principally from Orissa, and secondarily from Bihar and Bengal, and they live more in isolation than in an integrated social group. The basic population of the district is therefore formed by these six principal groups. They are all independent groups of people who in most cases, show cultural affinities.

The Santal, an Austric-speaking people, have now adopted Oriya as their second language, due to their contact with the Oriya-speaking people of the district of Mayurbhanj. Rev. A.S. Skrafsford, the author of the 'Traditions of the ancestors of the Hos or Santal people, (1887) and Sarat Chandra Ray, the author of 'The Munda and their country' (1912) believe that, the Santals are closely allied to the Munda groups.

The Santali language has been divided into Northern Santali and Southern Santali with some variations between the two. The Santali as spoken in Mayurbhanj district belongs to the southern group. Santali is a peculiarly expressive language as far as natural objects and things connected with the life of hunters or agriculturists are connected and has a delicate sense of humour. Their folktales are short, simple and of high literary value. They are orally transmitted from generation to generation. These stories are built round themes of love and hate. Most of the characters in them are human beings young and strong, struggling against forces of nature for existence. Besides these folktales, there is a richness of Santali folk-lyric generally in couplets and sometimes in more than four to six lines. In these lyrics we find thumb nail sketches of Santali life. They have a beauty of their own. Before independence the Santali writers had expressed their view in Roman ; Nagari, Bengali and Oriya scripts but at present a well-reputed Santali teacher Raghunath Murmu of Mayurbhanj (who is regarded as 'Guru gamke' a spiritual Guru) has invented a very peculiar script called 'Alchiki'. A number of poems, short stories, novels and dramas are now also written in that script and it creates a sense of patriotism among Santals.

There is a theological conception behind the beliefs of the Santals. Their supreme deity is 'Marang Buru' the creator and destroyer of the earth. Apart from this, they have several village spirits whom they worship in all public festivals.

Next in importance to Santals come the Hos referred to by the British enthnologist H.H. Risely, the author of the 'Tribes and Castes of Bengal' (1891) as Munda. They are also very early settlers of Mayurbhanj district. They also belong to an Austric-speaking group. According to 1981 Census 118534 persons in the district have 'Ho' as their mother tongue They like Santals, have a strong attachment for their language. They are known as 'Larka' or fighting Kols who were once noted for their jealous isolation of many years standing and long occupation of one particular territory and their contempt for all other classes that come in contact with them. The Kol tribes has given its name to the territory where it has made its home (Kolhan) and to the Kolarian family of tribes and languages. They are all second most numerous tribe of

Mayurbhanj. The Ho performs a very important social function by the help of 'Manki' the leader of the village. 'Munda' the priest of the vilage god and on the occasion of the anuual hook-swining ceremoney of a village, it is only he who ceremonially initiates a devotee. The Ho worship the Sun-God in the name of 'Singbonga' who is supreme and all powerful. There are other gods lower in rank like 'Burubanga', the Mountain God. The Chief festival of the tribe is 'Mageparab' held during the period of March-April, the occasion being the blossoming of the 'Sal' trees. There are other tribal gods who are worshipped on different occasions mostly connected with agricultural works. Their religious customs and social festivals show very little resemblance with those of Hinduism, because they have been living outside the Hindu fold from the very beginning. 'Birsa Munda' a great political and social leader of Singhbum district preached a new religion among them in the last part of 19th century as a result of which they got opportunities to be united and revolted against the British regime. The Hos are very sentimental and fond of songs sung by them at the time of their group dance called 'Jadui'. Of all the sentiments that inspire them for the use of poetry, the sentiment of love perhaps is the strongest as it is certainly the oldest. In fact this sentiment is as old as the human species.

Next in importance to Santal and Ho, come the Bhumija as far as Karma dance of Mayurbhanj is concerned. The Bhumijas take part in the dance in a large number partly because they form the third largest section of the population in the district. In 1981 Census 92,542 persons have been enumerated as Bhumija. They are mainly concentrated in the central part of Baripada subdivision. Risely believed that the Bhumijas are nothing more than a branch of the Mundas, who have spread eastward and mingled with the Hindus, and then for the most part severed their connection with parent tribe".

In Mayurbhanj the Bhumijas are known to be cultivators or agricultural labourers. They are Austric speaking people, and have now adopted Oriya as their second language due to their contact with the Oriya-speaking people of the district of Mayurbhanj.

The Bhumijas observe 'Sahrul Parba' as the Hos observe, 'Mage Parab' held during the period of March-April, the occasion being the blossoming of the Sal tree. They perform Saharae Parba during Diwali when cattle are worshipped by 'Dehuri', the priest. Like 'Nuakhia' another festival associated with nature is 'Phulpuja' which is observed before gathering of new leaves and fruits in the forest. In these ceremonies 'Dehuri' performs pujas to the village deities located in a grove. Some of the Hindu religious practices have been adopted in Bhumija-religion. They even require Brahmin priest for their marriage and death rites. The Bhumijas have no script at all. They express their views through Oriya script. Their folk-songs are especially sung at the time of Karma and Jadui dance which are very short, simple and of high poetic value.

Next in importance to the Santal, the Ho and the Bhumija, come the Bhunya, the Bathuri and the Gond—referred to by H.H. Risely as Dravidan tribes. They are also very early settlers of the Mayurbhanj District, though it is not definitely known whether they had occupied the country earlier than the Santal, the Ho and the Bhumija. Now the said Dravidian tribes who have completely abandoned their old tribal language or who are far on the way of doing so, in favour of Oriya as their mother-tongue. According to 1931 Census report the Bhunyas, Bathuris and Gonds, all adopted Oriya as mother-tongue.

The Bhunyas and Bathuries are chiefly found in Baripada and Panchpir subdivisions. Gait has described the Bathuries as one of the sub-castes of the Bhunyas while according to Russell the Bathuries although a subdivision of Bhunyas are regarded as inferior to them in social status. They resemble the Bathuries in their food habits, clothing and also in social manners and customs. They take fowl and also drink Handia—'rice beer' like Ho, Santal and Bhumijas. In their community, both adult and infant marriages take place. Divorce and widow marriage are allowed in their society. Their principal occupation was cultivation and preparation of 'Mudhi'. They perform Karma dance and Changu dance respectively at the time of rainy and in winter seasons.

The Gond is an important non-Arayan or forest tribe in Mayurbhanj. They as a race are marked for their simplicity, sobriety and honesty of character. The deities worshipped by the Gonds are Jangadeo, Lingadeo and Buradeo. These are worshipped to ward off sorrows and miseries. Their religious ceremonies are connected with various agricultural activities like ploughing, sowing and harvesting. Gonds are fond of Karma dance and Karma songs especially in the month of July and August.

Besides, the six important Scheduled Tribes of Mayurbhanj other forty tribes are also found scattered in the dense forest of Similipal and Suliapada. Most of them are immigrants from Chhotanagpur, Midnapur and Singhbhum. But all the tribes including the said six important tribes prefer to be called the permanent inhabitants of Mayurbhanj. They believe that Mayurbhanj is their original home where they still have their relations and kinsmen with whom they freely unite. In spite of their diverse traditions and languages there is a common socio-cultural bond which unites them together. At the time of makara parba, car festival and chaitra parba they not only get scope to be united among themselves but also avail opportunities to mix with non-tribal people.

Makara which is called the 'Sankranti Puja' is the biggest festival in the district observed by one and all. There is a saying that one may better pass on without a father but not without observance of makar. This is observed on the lst day of Magha, (mid January). On the occasion every one has at least a new cloth. The tribal people also have 'Handia' (rice bear) prepared and distributed among friends and relatives. The day following the Makar is observed as 'Bandar Nachha' (Monkey Dance). This concluding phase of the makar has great deal of mirth in all the houses. Puppet monkeys made of straw are made to dance from house to house. The Tusu songs are generally sung by the Bhumija and Bathuri girls and seldom by the caste Hindu girls also. Though there are rarely secular themes, most of the songs are still sung on the love episode. Among the folk songs besides Tusu, the most important 'Jhumar' is sung during the festival. Jhumar in this area is also sung in the course of a solo dance performed by a class of professional dancing girls known as 'nachuni' or 'Khemti'—meaning the same. Such songs are based on divine love of Radha and Krishna.

The Car festival of Baripade is very peculiar type and a little different from the Car festival held at Puri. The festival continues for three days. Thousands of Adivasis from Mayurbhanj, Midnapur and Singhbhum get together at Baripada by this time and enjoy a great 'mela' there with much pomp and ceremony. On this occasion sarees of better quality are worn by younger girls. The typical ornaments they use on the arms, ankle and the neck are made of brass and silver. In well-to-do families women cherish gold ornaments. Most of the women-folk never miss the opportunity of decorating themselves with whatever flowers are available in that time. The young men put on generally dhoti, kurta and a pagdi as head dress. They hold *dendra* in hand and sing love songs mainly addressing to the women-folk,

The chaitra parva of Mayurbhanj is very important in which the Hindus, the Scheduled Tribes and the Scheduled Castes people are equally interested. It is observed throughout the district especially at Baripada with great pomp and splendour. It falls in April when Simul, Kusum and Palas trees are in bloom everywhere. The local tribes mainly the Bhumija and the Bathuri have the 'pat puja' in the mid-April. The pat puja has essential similarities with the Bhokta ritual. In earlier days the Bhoktas used to roam the streets of the town of Baripada singing hymns in praise of Shiva and praying for the welfare of the king of Mayurbhanj. Today we see them at the end of this journey appearing around mid-night on the pandal where the popular Chhow dance is being performed. In Mayurbhanj Chhow festival is celebrated every year in the mid of April, this is also the time when Chaitra parba is celebrated by almost all communities and groups including Santal and Bhumijas. The Santals celebrate the 'Baha' or Flower Festival wherein they offer new flowers and fruits to the gods and goddeses before using them. Similarly the other groups and communities celebrate the Chaitra parba by way of Danda Nata, Chaiti Ghoda Nata and various other forms of folk songs and dances. There are various common elements in the ritual systems of Chhow and the other folk-dance items celebrated during this period. This only goes to emphasize the relationship between Chhow and the other folk and tribal dance-forms celebrated during the Chaitra parba in the adjoining areas.

Basically the origin of the Chhow dance links with many of the Adivasi dances like Baha, Dahar, Liran, Jadur and Ragnja. The drums, the mahuri and the flute used in the Chhow dance is akin to the use of the instruments in Adivasi dances.

Besides the festivals, the songs and the dances, the tribal people perform, they are more or less found to be artists by nature. When some one enters into their homes he will see the walls are painted with a variety of colours—white, yellow, black, red and chocolate, sometimes with one colour and sometimes with alternate stripes again with queer patches of triangles and rectangles. Various pictures, associated with their lives are generally found on the walls of houses.

Thus the Adivasis of Mayurbhanj, though they are not educated and advanced in their day-to-day lives, still have a great culture which we at the present time may believe or not, is survived and will be survived among them forever. They are simple, credulous and gullible people who even in the scientific age also believe in magic, witch-craft, spirits and ghosts. For generations, they have been exploited by the more organised econmic interests. Nowadays education brings about a certain awakening and often generates the courage to stand up them for their own right and even provides the means to imporve the conditions in which they live. Some Government programmes appear to have provided a scope to inject the maximum economic dose for removing the socio-economic backwardness of the vast majority of Adivasis, and help them to integrate themselves into the national mainstream of development and progress,

7

STUDY OF TRIBAL CULTURES IN ORISSA FROM DESCRIPTIVE DATA TO EXPERIMENTAL INNOVATIONS

Dr. F. M. Sahoo*

Orissa is a museum of tribal cultures. A number of tribes such as Kondas, Juangas, Sauras and Santals represent societal complexity and behavioural diversity. The study of tribal culture of Orissa is not a virgin area. During colonial days, foreign scholars like Elwin and Barley made rudimentary attempts to study tribal cultures. The post-Independence era has also witnessed attempts of anthropologists, ethnographers, historians, and other social scientists in the study of tribal cultures. Mohapatra, Mohapatra, and Nayak have studied Orissan tribals. All of these attempts are, however, guided by a descriptive approach where an indepth analysis of a particular tribal culture features as central concern. It is proposed in this paper that an experimental approach adopted to study at least two or more than two tribal groups would be useful in formulating laws of social science. Days of collecting butterflies are over; now there is a greater need to place tribal cultures in a framework akin to the chemist's notion of periodic

*Reader in Psychology, Centre of Advanced Studies in Psychology, Utkal University, Vani Vihar, Bhubaneswar.

table. The present paper asserts the importance and feasibility of such a pan-tribal enterprise.

Research Prospects in Orissan Settings

While there are bits and pieces of comparative data collected from Orissan tribes, there is greater need to bring together these scattered findings to a common framework. Social scientists need to understand the importance of an interdisciplinary approach. A better understanding of tribal cultures is possible only with the cooperation of anthropologists ethnographers, psychologists, sociologists, and other social scientists.

Apart from this integrative approach, a number of research areas appear to be a good candidate for comparative experimental studies.

It is well-known that tribals in Orissa are music-oriented. Songs and dances form an important aspect of their life. Although scholars have attempted to analyse songs and/or dances of a particular tribe no attempt to-date has been made to compare tribes on various dimensions of songs and dances. In other words, cantometric and choreometric studies would provide a wealth of information.

Another possible area of research involves the study of social deprivation. There are various tribal groups that differ in terms of culture contact. Acharya(1983) observes that Bathuda tribe in Karanjia is a tribe that inhabits in isolation, cutting itself off from the rest of the surroundings. Study of various psychological attributes of this tribe vis-a-vis a similar tribe without such deprivation can be undertaken to delineate the effects of deprivation.

The other side of the deprivation is acculturation. It is axiometic to maintain that many tribals are experiencing cultural changes that impinge upon them. Sometimes, the contact with a new culture, often the main-stream culture, places certain demands on the adjusting mechanisms of tribals. At a result tribals experience stress and strain in the process of coping with environmental changes. There are two plausible hypotheses that could be examined. First, investigations may be undertaken to examine whether the gap between traditional behaviour and new behaviour determines the amount of stress. Second, it is also interesting to determine in the insistence on adopting, the change is related to stress. It is hypothesized that people will experience greater discomfort longer is the journey people have to make from traditional behaviour to acculturated behaviour. Further, stress would be greater when the insistence that journey be taken up is greater. Cultural tribes could be appropriately selected to study such problems of acculturation.

A meaningful approach to cross-tribal research may include ecological factors as independent variables. Tribes can be chosen on the basis of their differences on these ecological dimensions. A number of ecological variables such as economic modes (hunting, gathering, agriculture), settlement pattern (nomadic versus sedentary), population size, social stratification, socialization emphases (assertion versus compliance) are possible candidates for cross-tribal research. The study of a single factor or combination of factors is possible by comparing two or more than two tribes differing on these dimensions. Berry (1976) and other social scientists have registered their impact by undertaking this enterprise in the West. In Orissan setting, use of tribal groups for unpackaging the effects of eco-cultural variables is a challenging task that lies ahead.

Apart from these suggested areas, other possibilities may also be explored. But in all cases, an important condition must be met before a comparison is undertaken. Tribal groups should be placed on a continuum of similarity, before their dissimilarity is examined and explained. We can interpret dissimilarity only in the light of similarity. Tribal groups in order to be comparable, must have some common features. Behaviours of people belonging to differing cultures must be functionally related to same problem. Further, concepts, tests, materials, and stimuli used for comparable cultures must be equivalent. Once the tribal groups are placed on a dimensional identity, comparison of differences can be interpreted scientifically. Considering the fact that Orissa is potentially rich with tribal resources, social scientists are likely to be enticed for future research prospects.

REFERENCES

Acharya, S.K. (1983). Personal communication.

Berry, J.W. (1976). *Human ecology and cognitive style : Comparative studies in cultural and psychological adaptation.* Toronto : Sage Publications.

Campbell, D.T. & Stanley, J.C. (1963). *Experiments and Quasi-experimental design for research.* Chicago : Rond McNally.

Das, J.P. (1961). *Ethnocentricism and stereotypes among Santalas. Journal of Social Psychology, 67, 79-84.*

Das, J.P. (1963). Authority pattern and family relationships in two primitive tribes of Orissa, *Eastern Anthropologist, 16,* 208-212

Durkheim, E. (1960). Quoted in H.C. Trionds and J.W. Berry (Eds.) *Handbook of Cross-Cultural Psychology* Vol. 2, p. 7.

Kobben, A. (1970). Comparativists and non-comparativists in anthropology. In R. Noroll & R. Cohen (Eds.) *A handbook of method in cultural anthropology,* New York : Natural History Press.

Leach, E.R. (1961). *Rethinking anthropology,* London : University of London, Athlone Press.

Mohanty, A.K. & Babu, N. (1983). Bilingualism and matalinguistic ability among Kond Tribals in Orissa, India. *Journal of Social Psychology, 121,* 15-22.

Parida, G. (1968). *Acculturation of Saura Children into Oriya Society.* New Delhi : Elite Publishing House.

8

ERADICATION OF MERIAH OR HUMAN SACRIFICE FROM THE SOCIAL LIFE OF THE KHONDS OF ORISSA IN THE 19TH CENTURY

Dr. Dandapani Behera*

From 1836 the British Government took prompt initiative and active measures for establishing close contact with the aboriginal Khonds and for suppression of their inhuman and cruel practices.[1] The suggestions and measures recommended by G.E. Russell the Commissioner of Madras Civil Service for dealing with the Khonds constituted the very basis of the Act XXIII of 1836. Under this Act, Ghumsar and Surada including the tribal tracts were removed from the jurisdiction of ordinary regulations and were placed under the special administration of the Collector of Ganjam, who was also designated as Commissioner for those territories being invested with Civil, Criminal and Revenue powers over them and to assist him an army officer was appointed as Assistant Collector being vested with military and revenue powers in times of emergencies, the latter would remain in the Maliah tracts for some months in a year to gain first hand knowledge about the Khonds, their traditional customs and problems.[2]

*Head, Dept, of History, Bhanja Nagar College, Bhanja Nagar, Distt. Ganjam.

Russell's Reports were based on his personal observation and on the evidences of the officers who accompanied the troops to the Khond tracts to capture the deposed Raja, Dhananjaya Bhanja and his family in February 1836, Captain Miller and Captain Stevenson of the 43rd Regiment of the Madras Native Infantry could manage to rescue 29 Meriah victims.[3]

In February 1937, Henry Ricketts, Superintendent for Tributary Mahals, reported to the Bengal Government about the prevalence of the same inhuman rite of Meriah among the Khonds of Baudh, and estate adjacent to Ghumsur.[4]

The Khonds believed that human sacrifice would give them good crops and protection against all diseases and natural disasters. They believed that the shedding of human blood was an imperative necessity for obtaining an excellent quality of the turmeric crop, which was an important product of the Maliahs. The Mariah victims were both male and female, irrespective of caste, religion and age [5]

The Meriah sacrifice was widely prevalent all over the Maliah tracts of Ghumsar, and Boudh and Daspalls, two neighbouring estates then in the Bengal Presidency, which together were known as the "Khondmals" extending over 2,500 square miles.

Another inhuman practice of female infanticide was also existing among a few tribes of the Khonds of the Maliah tracts.[6]

The Khonds performed the Meriah sacrifices particularly on the new moon days for propitiating the Earth Goddess with the offer of blood so that she would be pleased to ensure their prosperity and happiness and prevent all natural calamities.[7]

The practice of human sacrifice was carried on with the help of two classes of people, the Panas and Dambas, who supplied victims for sacrifices, these people kidnapped human beings mainly from the plains and sold them to the Khonds of high lands for sacrifice.[8]

Another class of people called the Janis, usually acted as priests on the occasions of the performance of human sacrifices.[9]

Edward Catsford referred to the practice of human sacrifice among the Khonds as early as in 1768. The British called this human sacrifice as "Meriah Sacrifice". Meriah was not a Khond term. Then British called victims of the sacrifice as Meriah and this term was perhaps a corruption of the Khond term "Mervi", which was the name of a Khond God called Mrivi Pennu, a brother of the Khond Goddess named Tari Pennu, the Earth Goddess for which the rite of human sacrifice was to be observed. The Khonds called the victims of human sacrifice as 'Toki' or 'Kedu', but not 'Meriah' as the British called them. T.J. Maltby stated that the British used the term 'Merria' not to indicate the "sacrificing Tribe", but to indicate the human victims of the sacrifice.[10]

The inhuman practices were in vogue among Khonds for over centuries owing to the inaccessibility of the tribal areas and to the indifference of the local authorities. Their supreme authority, the Raja of Ghumsar, had never questioned to the merit of the sacrifices and indirectly allowed them to continue. There were close contacts and relations between him and his Khond subjects for over centuries. It was when the zamindari was confiscated and the last Raja, Dhanjaya, his family and treasures were pursued into the Maliah territories, the British practically came to know about the Khonds and their practices and faced their rising in 1836, in support of their Raja's revolt against the Government, and initiated actions and measures against the Meriah sacrifice.[11]

In May 1837 Russel submitted his second report in which he mentioned that the Meriah sacrifice existed among the Khonds all over the Khond territory, especially in the Ghumsar Malliah and suggested caution in effecting the abolition of the Meriah sacrifice. Taking the vastness of the area into account, he emphasized that "we must not allow the cruelty of the practice to blind us", and wrote to Government to be cautious" to the consequences of a too much zeal in our endeavour to suppress it. The superstition of the ages cannot be eradicated in a day.[12]

He warned against any hasty measure of coercion and intimidation in the Khond tracts "which would arouse the jealousy of the whole race, possessing the strongest feeling of clanship". He emphasized on the exercise of moral influence and advocated against any exhibition of force. In his opinion, "the immediate suppression of the Meriah sacrifice could be possible if the whole of Khondmal was militarily overran and occupied, and that would involve Government into a war with a people with whom they had no connexion and no cause for quarrel.[13]

Russel was of the opinion that the Khonds would rise against the authority of the Government if they would be forced to give up an age-old custom which they thought to be a part and parcel of their religion. He emphasized his point by stating that "of the fearful sacrifice of life from sword and sickness, which would then ensure, there can be no doubt it is, I think more than doubtful, whether the desired objects could ever be attained by such measures. From all I have seen of them and known of their country, I feel I am convinced that no system of coercion can succeed".[14]

He suggested for establishing good relations based upon goodwill and understanding with the Khonds, and demonstration of any force and coercion, he feared, "would defeat that purpose".[15]

In December 1837 Captain Campbell, Assistant Collector. Ganjam, sought permission from the Madras Government to climb over the hills to persuade the Khonds to desist from the 'horrid practice' of Meriah, which was passed on to them by their ancestors over the centuries. Subsequently, the Madras Government granted permission to Captain Campbell to launch his expedition into the Khond tracts. He was asked by the Government to convince the Khonds in meetings of the inhuman aspects of the Meriah sacrifice by impressing upon them the point that the sacrifice was not at all necessary for their goodwill and welfare, and to prevent them from the conduct of the sacrifice not through 'coercion' but through 'Persuasions'. Accordingly, Captain Campbell made his entry into the Ghumsar Maliahs in December 1837, and rescued as many as 100 victims of the sacrifice.[16]

In 1837, when Captain Campbell first landed in the hill tracts for the suppression of human sacrifice, five or six of the oldest and most influential Khond chiefs together pleaded with him by saying : "We have always sacrificed human beings. Our fathers handed down the custom to us. They thought no wrong, nor did we. On the contrary we felt we were doing what was right. We were then the subjects of the Raja of Ghumsar. Now we are the subjects of the Great Government whose orders we must obey. If the earth refuses its produce, or disease destroy us, it is not our fault. We will abandon the sacrifice, and will, if permitted like the inhabitants of the plans sacrifice animal.[17]

From 1837 to 1840 Captain Campbell rescued 130 victims destined for the sacrifice during the course of his tour above the Ghats.[18]

On the 16th March 1841, Lord Eliphinstone, Governor of Madras, made the record of a lengthy minute in the council of the Fort. St. George, pertaining to the subject of the eradication of the Meriah sacrifice.[19]

Taking the enormity and frequency of the crime into consideration, the Governor, Lord Eliphinstone, gave his opinion in favour of Government's any attempt 'must be steady, progressive and systematic to cause the suppression of the Meriah sacrifice. He emphasized that: "the deep-rooted superstition of the whole nation should be eradicated with the least display of force".[20]

The Madras Council agreed with Governor, Lord Eliphinstone's suggestion that 'the best hope of success is in cautious and gradual measures, by which without any direct attack upon religious customs, the natural march of civilization might be surely facilitated.[21]

The Court of Directors of the East India Company in their letters to the Government of Madras, dated the 24th August 1842, readily approved of all the measures suggested by the Governor of Madras, Lord Eliphinstone.[22]

In 1841, the Madras Government appointed Captain William Macpherson as Assistant to Hannerman, then the Collector of Ganjam, who was also Governor's Agent in the district. Capt. Macpherson succeeded Capt. Campbell as Assistant Collector for Ghumsar and its Maliahs in 1842. He was assigned the work of suppression of the Mariah sacrifice in the Maliah tracts. On the 24th April 1842, he submitted his report to the Government. He reported that the Khonds carried the general impression that the Government would not take up "any decisive and comprehensive measure towards the suppression of the sacrifice" and "would remain satisfied with partial interference" in their affairs.[23]

In his report in may 1843, Capt. Machpherson mentioned about the rescue of 143 Meriah victims in that year itself. In his next report in July 1844 he referred to the prevalence of the female infanticide among the Khonds of Surada. He reported that they found no female child in many villages numbering over hundred houses in the Bori Mutha tract.[24]

It was not so easy to work out the measures against the continuation of the Meriah sacrifice because of the wildness of the tracts and the barbarous nature of their people. It was feared that any interference with the age-old socio-religious customs and practices would certainly set the whole of the Maliah highlands ablaze.[25]

Russell hold the opinion that "there is perhaps no subject on which we need to be more on our guard, lest our feelings should carry us beyond the bounds of sound discretion. They form a just opinion of its importance, and the line of policy which it is proper for the Government to adopt...I am strongly impressed with the belief that can be accomplished only by slow and gradual means."[26]

His observation on the measures for suppression of the sacrifice read:

"From all I have seen of them and know of their country, I feel convinced that no system of coercion can succeed; but on the difficulties of the undertaking by engendering fear and distruct, where it would be our endeavour to inspire confidence and goodwill...in my judgement, our aim should be to improve to the utmost, our intercourse with the tribes nearest to us the view to civilize and enlighten them and to reclaim them from the savage practice using our moral influence rather than our power".[27]

Lieutenant Hicks of the Bengal Army and Assistant to the Superintendent of the Tributary Mahals held a similar view on the Meriah sacrifice. According to him "the exercise of this revolting rite which Government is so desirous of repressing, owes its existence to the superstition of ages; this cannot be wiped from the ideas of the people in the space of a month or a year, even at the point of the bayonet; it is so intimately blended with their religion...but if the adoption of persuasive and conciliatory system be permitted for some time longer and officers employed in various parts of the country to gain information and report on its resources, it would allow the Khonds a sort of intercourse with us, and would go far to civilize and exalt their minds above their present low level, and would certainly be the means of lessening the frequency of the Meriah rite".[28]

On the 21st January 1837, Russell wrote to Ricketts that a large group of Ghumsur rebels had fled into the Baud territory and were received by Nabaghana Kohonoro, the powerful Khond chief of the region. Ricketts, immediately marched to Baud and met the Ghumsur Special Commissioner, Russell there. He heard from Russell that "an extensive system of human sacrifice had been discovered" among the Khonds of the Ghumsur highlands. He compelled Nabaghana Kohonoro to deliver up the Ghumsur rebels to Russell. He also rescued 24 victims who were kept ready for sacrifice to the Earth Goddess. In February 1837, he wrote to the Government of Bengal on the prevalence of Meriah sacrifice in Baud and Ghumsur hill tracts.[29]

In 1843, Macpherson reported Mills, successor of Ricketts about the existence of the horrid practice among the Khonds of Khondmals. Captain Ricks was appointed Assistant to Superintendent of the Tributary Mahals in 1843, he went to Khondmals to rescue the Meriah victims. The Khonds were not prepared to incur the anger of the Earth Goddess. Though they gave him a few Meriah victims, they kept many more with them and purchased many more for use.[30]

In 1845, at Calcutta, Macpherson drew up a scheme for the Agency for the suppression of human sacrifice and female infanticide.[31]

The Government in a Resolution dated 19th July 1945, decided to form a Meriah Agency to comprise the whole of the tracts where the customs of human sacrifices and female infanticide prevailed under the thought that the measures taken up in Ghumsur were bound to result in failure if immediate steps were not taken to bring all under one uniform system.[35]

Captain Macpherson, the Agent for Meriah Agency was held responsible for several mistakes committed in the concerned areas. He did not prevent the Native Assistants from exacting and oppressing the people in the name of suppressing the inhuman practices and resultantly, a climate of anger and discontent was built up all over the Khondmals against the Government.[36]

Brigadier-General Dyce was sent to command the troops and he took a totally different view of the steps taken up by Capt. Macpherson and within a week of his arrival expressed his opinion, so strongly to the Government of India that Capt. Macpherson and his Assistant Lieutenant Pinkey and Assistant Surgeon, Cadenhead were suspended and the charge of the Meriah Agency was given to General Dyce.[37]

A large number of Meriah victims were rescued by the

different officers of the Meriah Agency who traversed all the tracts of the Ghumsur Maliahs inhabited by the aboriginal Khonds, in between 1836 and 1845. The supreme Government initiated commendable measures towards the suppression of the horrid Meriah sacrifice through a band of sincere and selfless officers of the Meriah Agency and this heralded a new era of great humanitarian welfare and progress in the history of Ghumsar Maliahs.[38]

Thus, the practices of the Meriah was finally suppressed by both persuasive and coercive administrative measures of the Government.

REFERENCES

1. Mukherjee, P. History of Orissa, Vol. VI, Utkal University, 1954, p. 100.
2. Ibid., p.199.
3. Russell, Third Report, op. cit., pp. 57-58,
4. Russell, First Report, op. cit., p. 24.
5. Mukherjee, P. op. cit., p. 199.
6. H. Ricketts to Secretary, Judicial Department, Bengal 23, February 1837, B.R.A. Vol. January-June, 1837, No.396.
7. Ibid.
8. Russell, First Report on Ghumsar, 12th August 1835, p. 28.
9. Lieutentant Hill to Government, 18th December 1840.
10. Minute of Lord Eliphinstone, 16th March 1841, Madras Revenue Consultation of 1841.
11. Macleane, Manual of the Administration, Vol. I, p. 72.
12. Maltby, op. cit., p. 67.
13. Smoleth to Government, 6th September 1845: Madras Revenue Consultations, 1845.
14. Mukherjee, P. op. cit., p. 199.
15. Ibid.

16. Ibid., p. 200.
17. Russell, Third Report, op. cit., p. 55.
18. Ibid., pp. 57-58
19. Ibid.
20. Maltby, op. cit., p.75.
21. History of the Ganjam Maliah op. cit., p. 8.
22. Mukherjee, P. op. cit., p. 300,
23. Ibid., pp. 200-201.
24. Ibid. p. 201.
25. Ibid.
26. Ibid., p. 201.
27. Ibid.
28. Russell, Third Report., op. cit., p. 56.
29. Ibid., p. 55.
30. Ibid., pp. 57-58.
31. History of the Rise and Progress of the Operations for the suppression of Human Sacrifice and Female Infanticide in the Hill tracts of Orissa, Compiled from official correspondence from the year 1836 to 1854 (Calcutta), p. 82.
32. Henry Ricketts to Secretary, Judicial Department, Bengal, 23rd February 1837, B.R.A. January-June 1837, No. 396.
33. Mukherjee, P. op. cit., p. 202.
34. History of the Ganjam Maliahs, op. cit. p. 8.
35. Ibid.
36. Ibid., p. 8.
37. Ibid.
38. Mukherjee, P. op. cit., pp. 202-203.

9

THE PRACTICE OF INFANTICIDE AMONG THE KHONDS OF ORISSA

Shri Bhagaban Sahu*

Like Meriah Sacrifice, the Khonds of Orissa observed another inhuman custom known as infanticide, which was born out of their socio-religious superstitions during the 19th century. The Khonds of Orissa were divided into two great sects- the "Boora" Khonds and the "Tari" Khonds or, respectively the worshippers of Boora Pennu (the God of light, and the Tari Pennu (the Earth Goddess) on account of their religious differences. The human sacrifice was only prevalent among the Tari Sect while the practice of infanticide was confined to Boora sect alone. But among them this crime was frightfully prevalent, founded, as was supposed, originally on the idea, that the Sun God (Boora Pennu) contemplating the deplorable effects produced to the human race by the female sex, charged that "only so many should be preserved as they could restrain from producing evil to society".[1]

Only female infanticide was prevalent among some sections of the Khonds of Surada, Paddakimedi, Chinnakimedi and Ghumsar maliahs and Boudh-Khondmal subdivision of Angul district whereas both male and female infanticide

*Junior Research Fellow, Dept. of History Berhampur University.

prevailed to a very considerable extent in Jeypore and Rayaguddah areas.[2]

The reasons which led to this crime were many. But the expenses involved at the marriage rites was said to be most important cause of female infanticide.[3] According to Major Macpherson, it was forced on the people by the burden of their own marriage customs and their grinding poverty. A Khond brought his wife, paying in kind a sum equal to Rs. 50 to Rs. 70. Once married, a Khond woman had the right to leave her husband and go to another if she liked, and some exercised this right as many as half a dozen of times. When a Khond woman left her husband the latter had the right to demand from his father-in law the bride price, minus whatever marriage expense the latter had paid. The result of this system was that, anybody who had a married daughter was bound to refund the bride price for the discretion of his married daughter. Thus to a Khond, married daughter was a curse, and to the poorer and more ignorant Khonds the easiest way out of the difficulty was female infanticide.[4]

The Khonds justified the practice by a curious legend. In olden times, they said, there were four brothers, the sons of Donka Mallika, of whom three had eight sons each, while the fourth had two daughters. Not being able to find husbands, these girls cohabited with some of their cousins. As a punishment, their father was deprived of all his property by the other three brothers, and the guilty girls drowned themselves in a tank called Reda Bandh. After this, the three brothers were reconciled with their father, and as the quarrel between them was due to his daughters, they determined that thenceforth their female issue should be destroyed. Since then the famale infanticide came into vogue.[5]

Again, the Khonds believed that souls almost invariably returned to animate human forms in the families in which they have been first born and received. The reception of the soul of an infant into a Khond family was completed only after the performance of the name giving ceremony. The death of a female infant, therefore, before that ceremonial of reception was believed to exclude its soul from the chance of future female births in the family. And, as the first aspiration of every Khond was to have male children, this belief was a powerful incentive to female infanticide.[6]

Among Jannis and Dessaries (Priests of Khonds), it was a matter of social pride not to give a daughter to an inferior person. It arose out of a fit of temper of those religious people, and consequently took on a superstition colour and continued into posterity as a social custom.[7]

The Khonds' strong belief in astrology was another cause of infanticide—both male and female.[8] When a child was born, an astrologer, called Janny or Dessaury, was summoned and consulted by the parents as to the future prospects of the new-born infant. The astrologer constructed a horoscope or pretended to do so, and consulted a palmleaf manuscript called a 'Panji' in which were written certain sentences interspersed with rudely drawn figures of gods, goddesses, demons and devils, some of which were suposed to present good and some evil. After certain ceremonies the 'stylus' of bone or iron, used to write on palm-leaf was thrust into the 'Panji' and the figures to which it struck so fixed the fate of the child. If the god, goddesses or other sign represented good, the infant was spared; but if, it be one of foreboding evil, the doom of the child was fixed. The Dessary used to explain that the child if allowed to live, would be the source of evil to the father, mother, relatives or village community.[9]

Those Dessaries were generally of the Ooriah or Dooliah race, illiterate and ignorant men, who obtained their livelihood by working on the credulity and superstition of the Khonds.[10]

The living infant was then placed in a new earthen vessel, the mouth of which was closed with a lid on which a small quantity of rice and some flowers were placed, was buried. A fowl was then sacrificed over the spot. In some areas, the infant was not placed in an earthen vessel, but wrapped in a cloth and then buried.[11]

Whether it arose from pride or poverty, superstition or ignorance, the custom was a crime. The methods of killing the infants were extremely barbaric. At many places the child was destroyed immediately after birth by filling the mouth with cow dung or by immersing the head in cow's milk or by coiling the umbilical cord around the face. Another method was to administer a small pill of opium. Such were the cruelties associated with the customs of the Khonds.[12]

The life of no female children was spared, except when a woman's first issue was a female, and the head of the tribe desired to establish matrimonial alliance.[13] The number of new-born children destroyed annually was between 1200 to 1500.[14]

During the Ghumsar rising of 1935-37 the British Officers were 'first brought into direct contact and personal acquaintance with the Khonds'.[15] G. E. Russell, the Commissioner of the Madras Civil Service was the first officer to bring the news of female infanticide to the notice of the Government of India in 1836. Like Meriah sacrifice, it was also a matter of grave concern to the British authorities. They took both persuasive and coercive measures to stop the obnoxious custom.[61]

Campbell wrorked hard to stop the inhuman practice altogether. He explained to the Khonds and their Sardars the invaluableness of the said practice with the realistic support of the following sloka.

> "To kill one Brahman is equal to one hundred cows;
> To kill one woman is equal to one hundred Brahmans;
> To kill one child is equal to one hundred women;
> To kill one hundred children is an offence too greivous for comparison."[17]

In reply a group of Khond women told Campbell that they allowed the destruction of their female infants unwillingly in obedience to their husbands' orders and insistence. Many Khonds promised him that they would thenceforth rear up their female children instead of killing them in their infancy.

The rescued infants were sent to the camp of Christian missionaries. For some time the Government kept vigilance over the entire area. Instructions were issued to the British officials to count the number of the female children of each family of every village of the Khond tracts with a view to preventing them from destruction in future.[18]

In 1856, Dalhousie declared with satisfaction that the female infanticide was at an end. Credit goes to the British officers for having persuaded the tribal people to give up a crime 'sanctioned alike by antiquity and superstition' within so short a time.

REFERENCES

1. Browne, J.C., Indian Infanticide: Its origin, progress and suppression, (London, 1857), pp. 210-211.
2. Mukherjee, P. The History of Orissa, Vol. VI, (Cuttack, 1964), p. 497.
3. Campbell, J., Thirteen Years Service amongst the Wild Tribes of Khondistan, (London, 1864), p. 142.
4. O 'Malley L.S.S. Bengal District Gazetteers—Angul, (Calcutta, 1908), p. 26.
5. Ibid., pp. 26-27.
6. Browne, J.C., Indian Infanticide: Its origin, progress and suppression, (London, 1857), p. 211.
7. Chopra, P.N., Puri, B.N., and Das, M.N., A Social, Cultural and Economic History of India, Vol. III, (New Delhi, 1974), pp. 83-84.
8. Mukherjee, P., The History of Orissa, Vol. VI, (Cuttack, 1964), p. 497.
9. Bell, R.C.S. Orissa District Gazetteers-Koraput (Cuttack, 1945), p. 51.
10. Ibid.
11. Ibid., p. 52.
12. Chopra, P.N., Puri, B.N., Das, M.N., A Social, Cultural and Economic History of India, Vol. III, (Delhi, 1974). p. 84.

13. Correspondence, Captain Macpherson to the Agent to Governor, Ganjam, Berhampur, 24 April, 1842.

14. Russell, G.E., Report on the Disturbances of Goomsar, Dated 12 August 1836, p. 20.

15. Calcutta Review, Vol. V, January-June, 1846, p. 20.

16. Sahu, Bhagaban, Life of the Khonds of Orissa in the second half of the 19th century, M. Phil. Thesis, Berhampur University, 1983, p. 126.

17. Browne, J.C., Indian Infanticide: Its origin, progress and suppression, (London, 1857), p. 218.

18. Campbell, J., Thirteen Years Services amongst the Wild Tribes of Khondistan, (London, 1864), p. 142,

10

A STUDY OF THE SOCIAL AND HEALTH CONDITIONS OF "SAURA" TRIBE IN ORISSA

Dr. N.P. Mohapatra*

Introduction

The Saura tribe is one of the oldest primitive tribes of the world. They live in the eastern ghat region of Ganjam and Koraput districts of Orissa and Srikakulam district of Andhra Pradesh. The Saura tribe consists of many sub-tribal communities who can be easily identified by their distinct social customs, peculiarity of dress and mode of living and their employment pattern.

Historical Background

Although the Saura culture and civilization is very old, no comprehensive study about their health and hygiene has been made so far. The geographic situation of the Saura villages surrounded by hills and forests away from the main developed areas and lacking in communication facilities stood in the way of a systematic improvement of health and hygienic conditions of the community. They were believing fully (now also they partly believe) in the efficacy of divine blessing and magic of 'spirits' for cure borne out of the belief that due to

* Medical Officer (Eye Specialist), District Headquarters Hospital, Keonjhar.

wrath of spirits one suffers from disease or disability. They were offering rice, cloths, fowl, buffalo etc. to satisfy the angry spirit. They were worshipping different gods for cure from different diseases like 'amadi Soom' for gastro-entritis, 'Olaraba Soom' for Malaria fever, 'Jarada Soom' for intermittent fever, 'Panchal Soom' for suffering of young girls, 'Loba Soom' for safe delivery, 'Lurini Soom' for small-pox, 'Jana Soom' for better offspring. Previously they were worshipping the small-pox vaccines as Thakurani. After arrival of the Vaccinator with small-pox vaccine, they were allowing him to vaccinate only after the worship is over. Some of the people who are still superstitious are found in the community.

An isolated community away from the mainstream of civilization, lacked medical facilities curative as well as preventive. The Christian Missionaries in isolated pockets extended medical help to the needy and facilities provided by Government was too meagre. They suffered and died when they could not appease the 'angry spirit' and failed to get divine blessing..

The dawn of Independence is certainly a watershed in their life. Government undertook comprehensive development through Tribal Devlopment Agency and thereafter Integrated Tribal Development Agency, Parlakhemundi and as part of the programme health facilities flowed to the community.

Aim of the Study

An attempt is made to present a clear picture of health and hygienic condition of Saura community based on field study.

SOCIAL CONDITIONS

Residence

They usually reside in slopes of hills in low roofed cottages lacking in proper ventilation in a cooler climate. As the hilly region is in higher altitude communication facilities to the villages are still lacking. Climbing to a height (their Bagada area) is a daily routine. Many of them are in the habit of resorting to shifting known as 'Podu' cultivation in slopes and terraced lands. They leave their houses for 'Podu' area from early morning and return back to their houses by sun set. It is difficult to get an adult man in day time at his residence. This hinders the work of health workers (N.M.E.P., Leprosy, Family Welfare, Blind Control etc.) during their touring hours.

Literacy

Low literacy rate prevails among the tribals till today. Literacy rate of scheduled tribes in Ganjam district is 10. 8% as against the average tribal literacy rate of 13.9% in the State. Secondly, they have their own spoken language without scripts and alphabet. This stands in the way of explaining the basic health needs and hygienic point by the Health workers to them. Due to this language difficulty. the health extension programmes fail to achieve the desired result.

Income and Dietary habits

One's earning is directly linked with one's diet. Average land holding is very little and avenues of employment is too limited. Thus the purchasing power of a Saura family being small he suffers from lack of food. A survey in village 'Bhadragiri' of Srikakulam district revealed that for 165 days in a year the inhabitants lacked proper food. The protein content in their food is insignificant as they occasionally get protein from jungle or domestic animals and they are unable to supplement their diet with milk or pulses. Their habit of dry meat stored for days reduces the protein content of the meat. Besides they get very little vitamin from their diet. This results in damaging the proper functioning of the eyes, G. I. Tract and genito-urinatory system.

Chronic Alcoholism

Mostly the male members (many females also) of the Saura community are habitual alcohol drinkers which creates repulsion and irregularity of food habits causing damage to the body system.

Drinking Water

They usually drink water from spring and not from well and tube well (at present) but gradually they are becoming habituated to drink tube well water.

Belief in Spirit

As discussed earlier, the Sauras come to the qualified doctors at the late stage of the disease or disability after all their attempts to appease the spirits. At this late stage it becomes difficult on the part of Doctor to afford cure from the disease or disability. Costly life saving drug required in acute cases are not often available in hospitals and they being poverty stricken are unable to purchase them.

Difficulties in Undertaking Preventive Measures

As most of the Sauras are not available in their residential cottages during day times, DDT spraying for malaria mosquitoes on inner walls and roots of the houses are not possible. Immunisation of children against preventible diseases (Diphtheria, Tetanus, Whooping cough, Cholera, Tuberculosis, Polio etc.) are also hampered due to the same reason of non-availability of children in the houses during the visits of Health workers. This leads to a high mortality rate among Saura children.

Parameter of Study

In this study the Parlakhemundi Sub-Plan area of Ganjam consisting of Scheduled Tribal blocks with a population of around 2. 5 lakhs is taken into consideration. It is the result of observation in 8 Health camps, 13 eye camps, 10 school visits, 10 village surveys and 3 dental camps which were conducted covering all tribal blocks of the Sub-Plan area. Various important diseases were noted and treatment and/or advice given. In this study 6250 patients were included. Among them 3890 were non-tribals and 2460 were tribals. In age survey 900 tribals and 340 non-tribals were included.

Results of Observations

Table No. 1 is the disease pattern of tribal school children as compared to non-tribal school children in the age group of 5—15 years. Fig. No. 1 is its diagramatic representation. Fig. A is the diagramatic representation of disease pattern of tribal children only.

TABLE—1

Sl. No.	Disease	Tribals	Non-Tribals
1.	Scabies	25	23
2.	Spleenomegaly	9	4
3.	Malaria	6	2
4.	Worm infestation	5	10
5.	Avitaminosis	18	13
6.	Tuberculosis	1	3
7.	Anaesthetic Patch	2	1
8.	Caries teeth	15	18
9.	Trachoma, Betot Spots Phrynoderma, Nictelopia etc.	19	26
	Total	100	100

(i) Malaria and spleenomegaly seems to occur in tribal than non-tribal children This might be due to the fact that there is preponderance of malaria in agency area. The location of tribal villages, their habit of not taking proper treatment, inadequate and improper preventive measures taken up by the N.M.E.P. workers, spraying difficulties etc. contribute to the high incidence of malaria. It is observed that 54% to 67% of R.T. (Radical Treatment for malaria) being pending in the tribal district of Orissa.

(ii) Dental caries and avitaminosis appears to be more common in tribal than non-tribal children. Caries teeth occurs in children with calcium deficiency and avitaminosis combined with habit of uncleanliness and inadequate dental hygiene. It is rare to find a tribal child brushing with any kind of tooth paste and brush the teeth. They usually brush the teeth with the herbs available.

*For Figures see Appendix.

(iii) Various skin infections including scabies and infectations like ascariasis, ancylostoniastic etc. are less common in tribal than non-tribal children. Work infections are usually carried by vegetables and water which are contaminated. The tribal children are not regular vegetable eaters and drink water from spring which is usually non-contaminated. The symptoms of vitamin 'A' deficiency (xerosis, nictelopia, phrynoderm etc.) are less frequently seen in tribal children due to the fact that less number of them are infected with worms which causes this deficiency. Trachoma is also rare in tribal children.

Table No. 2 shows the disease pattern of tribals (both men and women) as compared to non-tribals. Fig. No. 1* is its diagramatic representation and Fig. B* is the diagramatic representation of disease pattern of tribals only.

TABLE—2

Sl. No.	Diseases	Tribals	Non-Tribals
1.	Anaemia	28	22
2.	Spleeno-megaly (malaria)	16	5
3.	Diabetes	0	2
4.	Hypertensions	2	8
5.	A.P.D. (acid peptic disease)	11	16
6.	Resp. infection	19	23
7.	Arthritis	6	8
8.	Obesity	0	3
9.	Ocular	6	8
10.	General debility neuritis etc.	15	15
	Total	100	100

(a) Anaemia, Malaria with or without spleenomegaly, general debility, features of neuritis etc. are more frequently seen in tribals than non-tribals. The reason might be due to the chronic infection with malaria and deficiency in the diet of the Sauras.

*For Figures see Appendix.

(b) Diabetese, hypertension, obesity and A.P.D. (acid peptic disease) are less frequently seen in the Saura community than non-tribals. The following might be the reasons.:

(i) Less intake of rich diet, rich carbohydrates and rich caloric diet.

(ii) They are mentally calm, they did not have any psychic imbalance, they are less worried and they get good sleep.

Psychosomatic factor plays an important role in causing these diseases.

(c) Respiratory diseases are less frequently seen among tribals than non-tribals. The reason might be due to the fact that the tribals remain away from dusty and smoky atmosphere, they get ample fresh air and their smoking habit is less than the non-tribals.

(b) Arthritis and arthralgia are less frequently seen in tribals than non-tribals. This is probably due to the active muscular work they perform in climbing and working in the hilly region throughout the year. It is observed that osteoarthritis is less frequently seen in persons doing active muscular exercise or practising Yogasana.

Table No. 3 is the ocular menifestations of tribals with comparison of non-tribals. Fig. III* is its diagramatic representation. Fig C* is the diagramatic representation of ocular menifestations of tribals only.

TABLE—3

Eye Disease Pattern

Sl. No.	Eye disease	Tribals	Non-tribals
1.	Mature cataract	90	180
2.	Immature cataract	101	215
3.	Trachoma	54	215
4.	Uveitis and Iridocyclitis	31	50
5.	Chronic conjunctivitis	102	273
6.	Refractive error	17	53

*For Figures see Appendix.

7.	Glaucoma	12	27
8.	Corneal ulcer	220	253
9.	Staphylloma & absolute Glaucoma	17	12
10.	Plthesis Bulbi	41	31
	Total	595	1308

(i) The total number of senile cataracts found in tribals are less than the non-tribals. This might be due to the reason that the longevity of tribals is less than the non-tribals (see Table No. 4). Senile cataract is mostly a manifestation of old age then forms of cataract like congenital, juvenile, complicated etc. do occur in tribal community.

(ii) Cornoeal ulcer, mature cataract, immature uveities, atrophic bulbi or plthesis bulbi, corneal opacity etc. are more commonly seen in tribals than non-tribals. The reason for this being that the tribals are more exposed to ocular injuries in forest areas which becomes extensive causing ultimate destruction of the eye. Secondly, they present themselves before the doctor very late after all their local attempt for treatment fails. Thirdly there are no qualified eye specialists available to tract them in their own area.

(iii) Trachoma is less frequently seen in tribal children but once it is contaminated, it spreads very rapidly among themselves (observations made among tribal girls at Chandragiri Kanyashram during 1979 and 1980). The low incidence of trachoma might be due to the fact that the tribal children are not vulnerable to dusty and smoking atmosphere and they get much fresh air and clean atmosphere.

(iv) Not a single case of diabetic or hypertensive ratinopathy was detected from the whole tribal series. The reason is due to the rarity of the parent disease among tribals.

(v) Absolute glaucoma with blindness are seen in comparatively younger age group with no obvious detectable cause.

Longevity

Table No. 4 shows the longevity pattern of tribals with that of non-tribals. Fig. IV is its diagramatic representation. Fig. D* is the diagramatic representation of the longevity pattern of tribals only.

Sl. No.	Age in year	Tribals	Non-tribals
1.	0—35	41	23
2.	35—40	20	23
3.	40—45	15	17
4.	45—50	12	14
5.	50—55	7	10
6.	55—60	4	8
7.	60 and above	1	5
	Total	100	100

In the tribal community maximum percentage of persons are found in the age group of 0-35 years. From 35 years onwards the number declines and a survival of more than 65 in tribal community is a rarity. This is a matter of concern.

HEALTH PATTERN

Certain peculiarities were observed in the health pattern of tribals.

(a) Cirrhosis of liver or alcoholic neuropathy and retinopathy were not observed among the Saura patients examined in the series though they are regular alcohol drinkers.

(b) Wound healing after operation is quick and perfect in tribal patients though they take less amount of protein and vitamins in their diet.

(c) Senile cataract appears at a comparatively younger age group i.e. in between 35 to 45 years of age.

(d) Absolute glaucoma with blindness is more common in younger age group without any detectable cause,

*For Figures see Appendix.

(e) Infant mortality rate in tribal population is higher than non-tribals although vitamin 'A' deficiency is seen to be less. It is reported that infant mortality increases in child with mild vitamin. A deficiency. Probably this is due to the infective diseases (diphtheria, tetanus, whooping cough etc.) that prevails amongst them with lack of proper nutritive care.

Improvement in Health and Hygiene

Although no remarkable improvement in health status of Saura community was noted in the short period of study (i.e., 1978 to 1982), however, the following facts came to light.

(i) Temporary blind cases (senile mature cataract) were decreasing from year to year. The number of mature cataract cases detected in the year 1981 was 116 as against the detection of 142 in the year 1980.

(ii) The people of that community were understanding the ocular and health hazards and as such it has been noted that they were coming for treatment of eye diseases in larger numbers than the succeeding years.

(iii) They were gradually coming for real treatment leaving aside the spiritual aspect of worshiping God for disease or deformity.

To achieve the full goal for the improvement of health and hygiene it requires longer period and even many decades.

Suggestions for Improvement in Health Status of Sauras

(1) Spread of the knowledge of the value of getting positive health and the modern methods of preventing diseases, by means of audio-visual aids is most important. The Health Workers should be from among those who can teach them in their own spoken language to create better understanding.

(2) The value of food and the necessity of balanced diet and vitamins should be explained to them by persistent propaganda through all possible means, so that gradually in future they will be interested to improve their diet content.

(3) They should be helped and motivated to take up poultry

and cattle farming so that they will be able to take milk and eggs regularly.

(4) Each of them should be encouraged to grow kitchen garden to get fresh green leafy vegetables regularly which will protect them from being infected by diseases.

(5) The benefits of hard work, taking fresh air, residing in airy, well ventilated houses, keeping the mosquitoes and flies out, for not drinking alcohol etc. should be taught in their own language and awareness about positive health should be created among all youngsters.

(6) Family welfare including mother craft (which includes baby care, timely breast feeding, maternal care etc.) giving protection against polio, diphtheria, tetanus, whooping cough, cholera, tuberculosis etc. should be encouraged.

(7) The benefit of all national health programmes should reach each family member to create timely awareness among themselves.

(8) The suggestive belief in 'spirit' in causing the disease or deformity should be removed by social education so that they will avail of medical facilities.

(9) The benefits of ideal planned family with proper time spacing in producing children should be taught by audio-visual media giving examples in benefits gained by the planned family and difficulties caused by unplanned family.

(10) 'Podu' cultivation should be discouraged as it damages the fertile soil which will lead to destruction of plantation, less rain, less production of crops leading to food deficit. For this government should develop lands and distribute them.

(11) Mobile medical facilities should be provided to wean them away from superstition.

(12) The village leaders' orientation and training camps should be organized frequently to enable them to understand the facilities provided by government. They should be shown developed areas so as to develop an urge in them to develop their conditions.

(13) Their economic status of the community should be improved. Massive and coordinated developmental programmes including horticulture, sericulture, coconut plantation, kitchen gardening, coffee plantation etc. should be taken up depending upon the geographic situation of the place. Piecemeal and isolated development programmes rarely can result in raising the economy of the community.

(14) More number of health workers should be provided with better facilities from mobility to work properly in the unapproachable areas.

(15) The local, national and international organisations (like Rotary Club, Lions Club, Jeyces international, Red Cross Satyasai Seva Samiti, N.S.S. Yubak Seva Dal etc.) should come forward to adopt at least one Saura village from each Panchayat in each year to raise their social and economic conditions as Government agencies cannot meet the problems alone.

Conclusion

The study is strictly on the basis of observations. The plantations are destroyed day by day from the forest areas by deforestation and Podu cultivation. The fertile soil is being washed out in larger amount year by year. The population of tribals is increasing day by day. It is hoped that this small article may help to attract the attention of the community.

REFERENCES

1. Dr. Mohapatra, N.P. Article on Health and Hygiene of Saura Community. Souvenir of Parlakhemundi I.T.D.A. of May 1984.

2. Dr. Mohapatra, N.P. Article on Ocular manifestation of Saura Community. Souvenir of Parlakhemundi I.T.D.A. May 1983.

3. Sri Das, A.B. Article on Social Life of Langia Saura, Souvenir of Parlakhemundi I.T.D.A. of May 1984.

4. Sri L. Tunga Article on Tribal Unemployment in Ganjam District.

5. Sommer A., Hussaini G., Tarwatzo I and Susanto D. (1983) 1:8350 : 586.

11

CHANGES IN SOCIO-ECONOMIC LIFE OF THE TRIBALS IN PHULBANI DISTRICT OF ORISSA

J.P. Kuanr* & S. Patel**

After India's Independence, the tribal situation has changed in its character. Before independence, the situation was of an ominous character due to discriminatory administrative policy which resulted in virtual isolation, imposition of sovereignty by the ruling power. Because of the inacccssibility to tribal communities, the local administration was in the hands of few privileged non-tribals, or the officials at the lowest rung of the administrative hierarchy who on the other hand exploited the tribals in more than one way. The British administration, in general, proved to be of suppression and neglect which bred dissatisfaction and discontentment in the minds of the tribals. The resentment of tribals took the shape of revolution in different parts of the country. Such revolts did not go unnoticed but resulted in the origin of Indian Council Act of 1861. Again in 1870, the British Parliament gave powers to the colonial government in India of legislation for regulating the affairs of the tribal areas under their administration. Later for the first time Scheduled Districts were formed in British Act

*Reader in Anthropology. Dept. of Anthropology, Khullikote College, Berhampur, Orissa.

**Reader, Government College, Phulbari.

XIV of 1874 and the term 'Scheduled Tribe' was used for the first time.

In the advent of India's Independence, the Indian leaders expressed their concern which was manifested in the Indian Constitution providing positive ameliorative safeguards. The Constitution laid down broad objectives which might bring radical changes in the tribal communities of the different parts of the country and since then Union Government has been leaning heavily on formulation of family-oriented programmes to raise the productivity of the tribals, particularly in the fields of agriculture, soil conservation and forestry. Most striking feature of planned changes as envisaged, are to involve people in the form of Community Development Blocks, Gram Panchayat and family who are directly affected.

The main schemes for the tribals were undertaken since 1952 under Five Year Plans. But these plans, until late, have been less serious and emphasis were laid on one aspect or the other and neglecting other aspects. The first Five Year Plan were undertaken for economic and educational development, improvement of roads and communications and the provision of medical and public health facilities. In the Second Five year plans emphasis was given on economic development in the fields of agriculture, cottage industries, forest cooperatives and setting up of special multi-purpose Tribal Blocks, the priority was given again to economic upliftment, education, health, housing and communication schemes. The Fourth plan came up with another programme, that is, of "area development approach", which envisaged the development of area in totality. It was expected by the Scheduled Areas and Scheduled Tribe Commission, that the total assimilation would be reached by the end of the Fourth Five Year Plan. Few pilot projects were started in Andhra Pradesh, Bihar, Madhya Pradesh and Orissa. The Fifth Five Year Plan incorporated different 'sub-plans' for total and integrated development of different tribal areas—larger tribal development areas by grouping TD Block and other small pockets of tribal communities. The Five year Development plans have been extended to the Sixth Five Year Plans in (1980-81 to

1985-86) since its inception in 1952. Thus the Five Year Plans have provided a broad framework for the nation and for the State for working out designs, techniques to bring over planning-efforts to the beneficiaries for a balanced future growth.

This paper is an attempt to highlight some of the consequences resulting out of such planned changes in the Boudh-Khondmals district. The district exhibits the highest concentration of Khond tribe in the state. (The word 'tribe' is here used loosely). The district Boudh-Khondmals is in Western Orissa and six other districts surround its boundary line. These districts are Puri in the east, Ganjam in south-east, Koraput in the south and Kalahandi, Balangiri and Dhenkanal canstitute the boundary line on the west, north-west and north respectively. The district is at an elevation of about 1, 700 ft. above the sea level. The three subdivisions Khondmal, Balliguda and Boudh constitute the district. Khondmal and Balliguda subdivisions constitute the larger part of the hill ranges and plateau markedly separated from Boudh subdivision by steep mountains. The two subdivisions, Khondmal and Balliguda, marked by high ranges of hills standing criss-crossed, narrow valleys, deep gullies, seasonal hill stream and small rivers, together have stretched an area of 8,365.57 sq. kms. of the total area of 11,094 sq. kms. of the total district.

The total population of this district is 7,12,772 (1981 Census). The name Khondmals can be attributed to 'MAL' (plateau), the principal home-land of the tribe Khondh. The Khond is one of the 62 tribal groups recognised as Scheduled Tribe. Out of the total tribal population of 50,71,937 which constitute 23.11% of the total population of the state, the Boudh-Khondmal district alone has a tribal concentration of 2,50,605 which is 40.31% to total population of the district. Out of the three subdivisions, the tribal concentration is very high in Khondamal and Balliguda subdivisions.

The predominant population of this district is the Khond, a generic name, which includes several sub-tribes. Though these sub-tribes show considerable racial affinity marked differentiation do exist in their economial, social and cultural life. These sub-tribes are the Kuttia, the Dongaria, the Penga and the Desia or Sasi Kandha. Their ralative isolation, local geographical condition held each of them to maintain an apparent ethnic boundary. The Kuttias are concentrated mainly in the western part of the Khondmals, in and around Kotagarha Block and Belghar Block. Besides, Kuttia inhabit in large concentration in the police station of Gudari and Chandrapur in the district of Koraput in close geographical proximity with the Kuttia of the Khondmals. The Petga, another sub-tribe of the Khond, inhabit the northwest part of Koraput, in the blocks of Kashipur and Kilyansinghpur. The Dongaria inhabit the hill tops of Nayamgiri of Rayagada and Gunupur subdivisions of the Koraput district between 83.50 E. and 83. 85 E. longitude and between 19.23′ N. and 19.40′ N. latitude. But the ethnographical features of the Desia Khond may be attributed to their exposure to outside world. These people are usually plain dwellers and their cultural life is that of the Oriyas, which is nearest to them. However all these subtribes are different from each other culturally and linguistically as much they vary in geographical and other extraneous factors like communication, education and above all exposure to urban centres. Though they seem to maintain a consistency in sharing the basic socio-cultural characters yet they have preserved the age-old traditions, beliefs and practices.

The tribal development is a central theme of the planners, who are concerned with sort of attaining the desired 'goals'. Again planners foresee a balanced growth through the schemes that they have devised. But the point is: is it aiming at acquisition of wealth ? or hoping for a technologically advanced and politically stable society ? At the present, it is difficult to conceive how to evaluate drastically a new social order when planners have several bottlenecks—social, economical, political, geographical and religious. Should the planners really claim to bridge up the gap between societies at different levels of development with millennia of tradition behind them ?

A planned change is bound to accelerate economic growth or social transformation. The economic growth in this area may be understood in terms of the agricultural productivity. It seems to be impossible to derive a development strategy suited to every condition. However, the plans and programmes have been impressive to encourage innovation not to isolate them from the mainstream of national life. This region is the real soil to test the results of the governments which is promoting social change and introducing new production at the local level.

The individual family in a village, which has been in a relatively strong footing of long standing economic growth does take some risk of experimenting in raising the agricultural productivity. Such families are able to afford to meet the expenditure of whatever little input required. Such families are making a living by tilling lands. But most of the families make a living working elsewhere for a considerable period in a year. This breeds a higher sense of social status in the former category of people over the other, although they generally form an agnatic group in a village and attempt to orient the life-style on the urban footing by acquisition of a radio-set, hanging few calendars, taking tea (mostly without milk), two times a day. Even status conscious, prevents some to allow their children to play with others. Till now, some have the firm conviction (level of aspiration) that they are destined to do, what their forefathers were doing.

It is observed that accumulation of property is given priority, because this helps an ambitious man in obtaining a following in the village. By lending paddy at the time of necessity, forms everlasting obligation. Thus accumulation of property increases personal freedom of physical, social and psychic mobility of the individual in a tribal society. Such mobility equips the individual with better awareness because of wider communication, which would back an individual to assert and impose the decision on the rest. Thus it impells an individual to secure power in the village political structure.

This has been leading to change in village level. On the other hand the development agents or the authorities who have been vested with power to look into the welfares of the people heavily lean on such persons, who show enthusiasm for developmental works, cooperates with the officials, looks into their comforts during their stay in the village. But they do so with ulterior motives to benefit themselves and their kinsmen alone, which is detrimental to the interest of the village. The people follows such persons under economic pressure and is obeyed from without rather from within.

Therefore the harmony of the community life is bound to decline. A community may designate localities with populations ranging from few hundreds to several millions, but the goods should be delivered to each one of them through such developmental movements. The project accomplishments must not be expressed through mere statistical targets but must be understood as a way of life as conceived by the planners. The differential economic growth frustrates the very spirit of the developmental policies which envisage a "balanced growth".

Peoples' growing distrust in the agents is the greatest barrier in forging ahead the developmental activities. In 1974, the officials pushed the fertilizer along with the free distribution of food-grains. They were given with the understanding that the fertilizers too were free gift packages. But surprisingly, the cost of the fertilizer was realised after a couple of years. However the strategy (if we call it so) could have been thought in terms of "sequences and priorities", so that the fertilizer could have been utilised instead of breeding in the people's mind the sense of distrust. There are many a force why the people show a general apathy towards the developmental programmes.

There are some conflicting situations between the developmental programmes and the values, belief, ethics of the people. But there has been a greater reconciliation now than the past few decades which cannot be understood as in a fluid state. These tribals still count on rituals with regard to good productivity fertility of land, growth of population and physical well-being. The Khond may have formal education, but have survived through generations adjusting themselves with the surrounding environment. This has been possible because, of their intelligence and ability of adjustment with the surroundings. So also, they may be able to cope with the modern programmes of development only when they are still not kept ignorant about such new opportunities made available to them. Some via media are to be evolved to allow the people to do themselves free from imposition or compulsion from the know-how from capital cities. Thus, development can bring forth development of individual personality, perception and awareness which will build a confident individual.

REFERENCES

Bhattacharya, D. (1975). 'India's Five-Year Plans : Analysis, Progressive Publishers, Calcutta.

Chaudhuri, B. (1982). 'Tribal Development in India : Problems and Prospects'. Inter-India Publication, New Delhi.

Pattanaik, S.C. and S. Patel (1982). 'Impact of modernization on tribals: Economic dualism and path of change'. Utkal Economic Papers, Vol. 1, No. 1, p. 13.

Planning Evaluation Organization (1958). 'Fifth Evaluation Report'.

Roy-Burman, B.K. (1965). Cultural factors in economic development and technological change in tribal India'. Jr. of Soc. Res. B; 1:21-32.

Singh, B. (1977). Tribal development at cross-roads : A critique and a plea'. Man in India, Vol. 57, No. 3, Jul-Sept.

12

INDUSTRIALIZATION AND CHANGING PATTERN OF SOCIO-ECONOMIC LIFE OF TRIBALS—A CASE STUDY IN THE LATHIKATA REGION OF SUNDARGARH DISTRICT

Dr. Basudev Sahoo* &
Shri Ajay Kumar Mohapatra**

Industrialisation entailing urbanisation is a powerful tool of development and exercises perceptible influence on social fabric. Peculiarly enough, most of the big industrial projects are established in those areas which are predominantly inhabited by the tribal people. The reason is obvious: the primary need of the basic and key industries, the minerals, are abundantly available in these areas. Accordingly, the nation's first public sector Steel Plant was established in Rourkela in the mid 1950s. The process of industrialization in this region received an impetus further with the setting up of various other ancillary and subsidiary industries. Lathikata, a small obscure tribal hamlet at a distance of 20 kms. from Rourkela has thus come into prominence after the establishment of the Orissa Industries Limited in 1963. The industry was started with a capital investment of Rs. 52 lakhs and an annual installed capacity of 34,000 tonnes of refractories.[1]

*Professor of Economics, Ravenshaw, Cuttack.
**Lecturer in Economics, Government College, Angul.

The establishment of an industrial complex is bound to effect perceptible changes in the life of the individual, family society and the entire environment. These changes are clearly visible in the social, economic and psychological life of the tribals of the Lathikata region.

The Oraon and Munda are more numerous tribes in the Lathikata region. They are "Social groups with a definite area, dialect, cultural homogeneity and unifying social organisation."[2] They generally constitute relatively a closed society. As D.L. Sills points out, "Ideally tribal societies are restricted in the spatial and temporal range of their social, legal and political relations and possess a morality, religion and world view of corresponding dimensions."[3] The economic relations are also of subsistence type. The existing technological knowledge is utterly primitive, belonging to a very low level.

Under such a background of the tribals in general and the Oraon and Munda communities in particular, it is interesting to note the changes concerning their socio-economic life.

Objectives of the Study

The present study aims at the following objectives:

(i) To show the economic changes i.e., changes in occupation, income pattern of expenditure, indebtedness, savings, entrepreneurship and the life of the tribals.

(ii) To show the socio-psychological and attitudinal changes in family structure, marriage, education, health care, food habits, attitude towards modern living, leisure and recreation, group living and the like of the tribals.

Methodology

The study is based upon the household survey method by means of prepared questionnaires. Sixty households in all have been selected by random sampling method. For an objective comparison of the socio-economic changes between tribals and non-tribals, the sample has been equally divided into two parts, viz., thirty households (50%) belong to the non-tribals. Personal interview method has been adopted by interviewing the heads of the households for collecting the required information. For a suitable comparison of socio-economic life between past and present, '1963' has been chosen as the 'cut off' year because the ORIND at Lathikata was set up in that year.

The survey work actually started during the later part of 1983 and was completed during the earlier part of 1984.

The Study Area

The sample households are situated in two neighbouring villages of Lathikata and Hatibandha. Both the villages belong to the Lathikata block of Sundargarh district. Lathikata with a total population of 981 and comprising 255 households is located at a distance of 20 kms. from Rourkela. The total area of the village is 1336 acres including 95 acres as forests. Rice is the staple crop grown in the village. Of the total population, 371 or 37.81% are tribals.

The village Hatibandha with a population of 1,354 and consisting of 259 households is situated at a distance of 9 kms. from Lathikata. The total area of the village is 827 acres including 46 acres of forests. Rice and ragi are the main food crops of the village. Of the total population 1,030 or 76.07% are tribals.

Findings of the Study

1. Change in Occupation of the People

Before industrialization, i.e. before 1963, 46.66% of the tribal households depended on agriculture, another 46.66% earned their livelihood as agricultural labourers and the rest 6.66% depended on other types of labour. A significant change in the occupation of the tribals is clearly noticeable at present when only 6.66% of them depend on agriculture, 73.33 depend on services and the rest 20% depend on other types of labour. This change in occupation is due obviously to industrialization which opened up avenues for services and labour (See Table-1).

So far as the non-tribal households are concerned the trend of changes in occupation is almost the same, i.e. from agriculture to services albiet 13.33% of them depending on business and trade at present (See Table-2).

Taking into account the changes in occupation in three generation levels of the tribals, it is found that agriculture and agricultural labour occupied the main sources of livelihood of the grandfather's and father's generation. But in the present generation, it is the services and other industrial labour which are the main occupations. The trend of occupational changes in regard to the non-tribals house-holds is almost the same, i.e., from agriculture and agricultural labour in the grandfather's and father's generations to services in the present generation. But in case of non-tribal households they are spread over almost all categories of occupation including trade and commerce (see Table 3).

2. Change in Income

Before industrialization the annual income of about 93.33% of the tribal households was below Rs. 2000/-but at present the level of earning has increased manifold so much so that 73.33% of them are now earning an income between Rs. 5000/- and Rs. 10000/- (Table 4). No tribal household earns income exceeding Rs. 10,000/-.

The income position of the non-tribals is slightly better in both the periods. About 20% of them earns more than Rs. 10,000/- per annum, and about 80% of them earn between Rs. 4,000/- and Rs. 10,000/- (See Table 5).

3. Change in the Pattern of Expenditure

Before industrialization, all the tribal households were spending up to 90% of their income on food. No household was spending anything on education of children, books and magazines and house rent. But at present the share of expenditure on food has visibly declined and they are also spending on the above items.

4. Indebtedness

According to the survey, 20% of the tribal house-holds made loans before industrialization mainly from money-

TABLE 1

Distribution of the heads of the S.T. Households according to their occupation before industrialization and at present

Occupational categories	Before Industrialization		At present	
	Number of heads of households	Percentage	Number of heads of households	Percentage
Agriculture	14	46.66	2	6.66
Agricultural Labour	14	46.66	—	—
Forest Labour	—	—	—	—
Unskilled labour Other than agriculture	2	6.66	6	20.00
Service	—	—	22	73.33
Business and trade	—	—	—	—
Miscellaneous	30	100.00	30	100.00

TABLE 2

Distribution of the heads of the Non-S.T. Households according to their occupation before industrialization and at present

Occupational categories	Before Industrialization		At present	
	Number of heads of households	Percentage	Number of heads of households	Percentage
Agriculture	14	46.66	4	13.33
Agricultural Labour	8	26.66	—	—
Forest labour	—	—	—	-
Unskilled labour Other than agriculture	—	—	—	—
Services	—	—	20	66.60
Business and trade	2	6.66	4	13.33
Miscellaneous	30	20.00	2	6.66
Total	30	100.00	30	100.00

TABLE 3

Occupational distribution of S.T. and Non-S.T. Households at different generation levels

Occupational categories	S.T. Households						Non-S.T. Households					
	Ego's grand father		Ego's father		Ego		Ego's grand father		Ego's father		Ego	
	No.	%	No.	%	No.	%	No.	%	No.	%	No.	%
Agriculture	18	60.00	18	60.00	2	6.66	16	53.33	14	46.66	4	13.33
Agricultural Labour	10	33.33	8	26.66	—	—	6	20.00	2	6.66	—	—
Forest Labour	—	—	—	—	—	—	—	—	—	—	—	—
Unskilled Labour other than Agriculture	2	6.66	4	13.33	6	20.00	4	13.33	8	26.66	—	—
Service	—	—	—	—	22	73.33	2	6.66	4	13.33	20	13.33
Business and trade	—	—	—	—	—	—	—	—	—	—	4	13.33
Miscellaneous	—	—	—	—	—	—	2	6.66	2	6.66	2	6.66
Total	30	100.00	30	100.00	30	100.00	30	100.00	30	100.00	30	100.00

TABLE 4

Annual Income of the S.T. Households before Industrialization and at present

Annual income of the households (Rs.)	No. of households before industrialization	%	No. of households at present	%
Below 1000	14	46.66	—	—
1001—2000	14	46.66	2	6.66
2001—3000	—	—	—	—
3001—4000	2	6.66	4	13.33
4001—5000	—	—	2	6.66
5001—6000	—	—	6	20.00
6001—7000	—	—	4	13.33
7001—8000	—	—	2	6.66
8001—9000	—	—	6	20.00
9001—10,000	—	—	4	13.33
10,000 and above	—	—	—	—
Total	30	100.00	30	100.00

TABLE 5

Annual Income of the Non-S.T. Households before Industrilization and at present

Annual Income	No. of households before industrialization	%	No. of households at present	Percentage
Below 1000	8	26.66	—	—
1001—2000	20	66.66	—	—
2001—3000	2	6.66	—	—
3001—4000	—	—	—	—
4001—5000	—	—	6	20.00
5001—6000	—	—	8	26.66
6001—7000	—	—	2	6.66
7001—8000	—	—	4	13.33
8001—9000	—	—	2	6.66
9001—10000	—	—	2	6.66
10000 and above	—	—	6	20.00
Total	30	100.00	30	100.00

lenders at the rate of interest ranging from 16% to 20%. At present the percentage of loans remains the same as 20%. But loans are mainly made from Government agencies like LAMPS and relatives. Loans are incurred by the tribals for meeting personal expenses. They are hardly utilized for productive purposes like improving lands or investing in business. So far as non-tribal households are concerned, 13.3% of them incurred loans principally from money-lenders at not less than 16% rate of interest. At present the percentage of debtors has increased to 40%. The purpose of loans is mainly for meeting personal expenses like marriages and festivals although some of them have invested in business.

5. Saving and Insurance

Before industrialization, only 6.66% of the tribal households saved and they saved mainly for purchase of property. 93.3% of them did not save at all. But at present, the percentage of savers has increased to 26.6% and they save for varied purposses like education of children and security in old age, etc. None of the heads of tribals households has invested in insurance schemes.

So far as non-tribals are concerned they saved nothing in the past. However, at present the percentage of savers has increased to 20% out of which 6.66% are saving in the insurance policies.

6. Family and Marriage

Out of the thirty tribal households, ten households (33.3%) are of joint type and the rest 20 households (66.6%) are of nuclear type. All the heads of the joint households are of the view that the main reason of their adhering to joint families is familial affection. So far as the heads of the nuclear family for it avoids friction and the rest 60% support it because it minimises economic burden.

Twenty per cent of the total tribal households are of small size (2-3 members), 53.3% are of medium size (4-6 members) and the rest 26.6% are of large size (7 members and more).

Of the total tribal households, 66.6% are of the view that sexual relation is the greatest attraction of marriage, whereas 6.66% hold economic participation, 20% hold legal contract and the rest 6.66% hold emotional interdependence as the greatest attraction of marriage. Moreover, all the household that monogamy is the most preferable marriage system.

As regards the non-tribal households, 26.6% of them are of joint type and the rest 73.3% are of nuclear type. It is the familial affection which is the main reason for adhering to joint family. For nuclear type, 73.33% hold that it minimises economic burden and the rest 26.66% hold that it gives greater freedom to couples.

Of the total non-tribal households 26.6% are of small size, 46.6% are of medium size and the rest 26.6% are large families. Similarly 73.33% are of the view that sexual relation is the greatest attraction of marriage, whereas 13.33% hold economic participation and the rest 13.33% hold legal contract as the greatest attraction of marriage. All the non-tribal households support monogamy as the best marriage system.

7. Education

Eighty per cent of the tribal households are in favour of sending their sons to school and 66.6% of them support their daughters' schooling. Similarly 53.33% of the heads of households answered that education is necessary for securing employment and 33.3% of them answered that education is necessary for broadening the outlook. The rest 13.3% did not answer at all.

The survey shows that only 13.33% of them spend on the purchase of books, papers and magazines. It is revealed that 40% of the tribal heads are illiterate, 13.3% have read up to primary level, 26.6% up to High school level, 13.3% are matriculates and 6.66% are undergraduates.

Of the non-tribal households, 93.33% desired their sons to go to schools and 66.6% of them favoured their daughters' education. Asked about the necessity of education, 13.33% answered that education is necessary for social and cultural adjustment, 60.80% of them thought it necessary for securing employment and 26.66% for broad outlook.

Among the non-tribal households,40%spend on the purchase of papers, books and magazines. 26.66%of the non-tribal heads are illiterate, 13.33% have read up to primary level, 6.66% up to M.E. level, 20% up to high school level, 20% are matriculates and 13.33% are graduates.

8. Health and Family Planning

At present, 86.6% of the tribal households treate their patients in hospitals. Only 6.66% among them consult local herbalists and the rest 6.66% approach priests or ojhas for treatment of their patients.

An many as 80% of the households feel that family planning is a good method for controlling the growth of population and the rest 20% are not conscious of it. However, among, the tribal families nobody has adopted family planning.

So far as non-tribal families are concerned all of them treat their patients in hospitals and they consider family planning essential to check population growth.

9. Food Habits

According to the survey, the food habits of 46.66% of the tribal households have changed due to the emergence of industrialization. Previously their staple food crop was maize or jawar, but today they have changed over to rice or wheat. Similarly they are now taking fish and meat intermittently.

Among the non-tribal households, the food habits of nearly 80% remain the same, whereas the rest 20% have changed their food habit due to rise in the levels of income.

10. Beverages and Intoxicants

Nearly 73. 3% of the tribals at present are accustomed to

taking tea in contrast to only 26. 6%.previously. Similarly 66. 6% of them were taking liquor habitually or occasionally before industrialization, but at present their percentage has come down to 53. 3%. As regards the reasons for their addiction 60% of them attribute it to tradition, 30% to self-medication to relieve pain and the rest 10% take to liquor to relieve emotional distress.

Among non-tribal households, the percentage of tea-takers is higher at 86. 6% as against 66. 6% in the past. In contrast to the tribal households, none of the non-tribal heads of the households consume liquor or other intoxicants.

11. Leisure and Recreation

Among tribal households, 93. 3% spend their leisure in visiting their friends, 13.3% in visiting pictures, 20% in reading and 26. 66% in listening to radio. Similarly 93. 3% are satisfied with the amount of leisure that they are getting in an industrial atmosphere. 13. 3% of them are members in library and club.

As regards the non-tribal household, 80% spend their leisure in visiting their friends, 13. 33% in visiting cinema-houses 40% in reading and 20% in listening to radio. 80% of them are getting adequate leisure and 13. 3% of them are members in library and club.

12. Group Living and Neighbourhood

All the heads of the tribals households reported that they got maximum help from their kinsmen during the observance of ceremonies like birth and marriage etc. 13. 3% of them answered that people of other castes and tribes were joining their ceremonies before industrialization. Presently also, the same number of heads of households receive people of other castes and tribes in their ceremonies. So far as the relationship among the neighbours is concerned, all the tribal heads (100%) reported to have cordial relations.

Among the non-tribal heads, 93. 33% get maximum help from their kinsmen and only 6. 66% get help from neighbours, during ceremonies. 20% of them said that people of other castes and tribes were joining their ceremonies both before industrialization and at present. All the non-tribal informants reported that their relationship with neighbours is cordial.

Conclusion

From the findings it is clear that there has been a significant change in occupation from traditional agriculture to services in the industrial complex during the last two decades. This change is almost similar to both tribals and non-tribals. But some of the non-tribal households hold business and trade as principal occupations whereas no tribal household has adopted such occupation. Thus entrepreneurship has not yet developed among the tribals.

A comparison of the levels of income of the tribals and non-tribals shows that the latter's earnings in both the periods are higher than those of the former. Thus, it appears that the share of relative earnings has gone more in favour of the non-tribals.

So far as the change in the pattern of expenditure is concerned, both the groups are spending on non-traditional items like education of children, transportation, medical treatment, purchase of books and magazines and the like at present. This is due largely to the advent of industrialization and consequent spread of education and mobility of labour. Another trend quite evident from the findings is that with the rise in the level of income, the proportion of income spent on food goes on declining since the additional income is diverted more than proportionately towards other items.

As to the indebtedness, the number of debtors among the tribals remains the same in the two periods in question. As against this the percentage of non-tribals debtors have increased quite visibly. And as far as saving is concerned, the number of tribal households who have saved, exceeds that of non-tribals. However, some of the non-tribal households have saved in the insurance policies but not tribal household has done so. It is thus clear that the non-tribals in this area are worse savers than the tribals.

Industrialization has also made a delve into the individual and social life of the people around the region. It is observed that the joint family system of the tribals is gradually giving way to nuclear family system and while preferring a nuclear family, they are more guided by economic considerations. Similarly, with the disintegration of the joint family system, most of the tribal households (nearly 80%) are of small and medium size today. So far as marriage is concerned most of them attach more importance to sexual relation as the greatest attraction of marriage, and all of them are in support of monogamy. Most of the non-tribal households today are also of nuclear type and this is because it minimises economic burden. And consequently most of the families are of small and medium size.

The study indicates that education is gradually spreading among the tribals. Most of the households do send their children to schools today and for them the necessity of education arises due to its employment potential. However, most of them (about 86. 6%) do not spend anything on the purchase of books and magazines. The leval of education and expenditure on books etc., on the part of the non-tribals are, however, higher.

The majority of tribals no longer get their diseases treated under the herbalists and priests. They go to the hospital for treatment. Most of them are also conscious of the advantages of family planning, although nobody among the sample households has adopted this method. But among non-tribals, all heads of the households treat their patients in modern hospitals. All of them are conscious of the need for family planning and some of them have adopted it aslo.

With the emergence of industrialization and consequent rise in the levels of income, the food habits of the tribals have undergone a change. They have switched over to superior varieties of food grains like rice and wheat and some of them consume meat, fish and eggs regularly at present. Similar change in the food habits has also occurred in case of non-tribals.

The percentage of tea-takers among the tribal has registered a perceptible increase from 20% to 80%, while the percentage addicted to alchohol has decreased slightly. Among non-tribals, the percentage of tea-takers is even higher in both the periods. Nobody among the sample households takes to intoxicants habitually.

Most of the inhabitants, tribals and non-tribals alike, get enough leisure and spend it in various ways like visiting friends, going to cinema, reading and listening to radio. In fact tribals constitute relatively a free society and it is held that an industrial set up with its hardship of routine-bound life cannot bind the tribals easily. But it is seen from the sample households that the tribals in particular are well adjusted to the new environment. They do not reveal any discontentment at the changed environment.

It is also found from the survey that all the households (both tribals and non-tribals) live as good neighbours in an atmosphere of cordiality and mutual help. Group living as evinced in collective enjoyment at festive occasions is not marred by caste or religious differences.

Thus the tribals in Lathikata region are gradually adapting to the new surrounding of an industrial society. Fortunately or unfortunately the tribal codes and ethos are not observed as rigidly as before. Cultural intermixture between the tribals and non-tribals is on the increase and this is sure to effect a perceptible change in the life style of the tribals.

While most of the changes reflecting modern and scientific attitude are welcome, attention has to be paid to preserve and promote the virtues of tribal life, such as honesty, integrity, fellow feeling and respect for the elderly persons. The art and culture of the tribals, songs, dances and the like may be given new orientation and respectability in the overall scheme of cultural development. Definite measures have to be taken to enlist the participation of the tribals in trade, commerce and industry, so as to minimise the gulf between the tribals and non-tribals and remove any trace of exploitation.

REFERENCES

1. Senapati, N. and D.C.Kuanr (ed.) Orissa District Gazetteer, Sundargarh, Government of Orissa, 1975, p. 173.

2. Kerkel G.L. "Social Change in Tribal India"—Development Policy and Administrative Review (Jan-June '77).

3. Sill D.L. (ed.)—International Encyclopaedia of the Social Sciences-Vol. 15, The Macmillan Company and Free Press, New York, 1972, p. 146.

13

AN ANALYSIS OF THE IMPROVED ECONOMIC LIFE OF THE TRIBALS OF ORISSA AND THE WAY TOWARDS INTEGRATION

Dr. U.C.Mohanty*

Never had there been such a massive attempt in the history of India to improve and integrate tribal communities as it is done in the post-Independence era. Not only protective safeguards have been provided in the Constitution of India, but it also ensures the provision of financial grants from the consolidated funds of the State. Yet decade after decade such protective discriminations are further extended which leads to the suspicion whether there is any possibility of ameliorating and improving the tribal situation in India. At this stage there is urgent necessity of evaluating how far the tribals have improved their economic conditions and how far they have been integrated within the larger Indian society. But prior to such discussions a brief delineation of the nature and features of tribal societies and the very definition of tribes may not be out of context.

Who are the Tribes

A question that arose during the national movement for

*Department of Anthropology, University of Madras.

independence and which was more discussed at the academic level during post-Independence era was what is the proper definition of Indian tribes and how far they differ from castes. There have been lot of discussions on this issue but various definitions put forward are not only different, but they are also highly contradictory and confusing. Yet the best, at least indisputable, definition of Indian tribes refers to those communities which are declared as such by the Constitution of India. But before declaring a community as a tribe along with others usually two criteria are emphasised, that of poverty and isolation. The tribal people are segregated from the general population due to their ecological conditions. They usually live in hilly or forested area usually in inhospitable climate. Due to such physical conditions the process of culture contact becomes slow that leads to backwardness of tribal communities. In Indian situation due to social inhibitions and due to ideas of purities and pollution of caste society, the tribal communities are further disadvantaged which arrests their upward movement. Secondly the tribal peopie are inextractably poor. Through historic process they have been pushed to more infertile areas and whatever they produce or gather with great expenditure of time and energy are whisked away through the trickery of traders, money-lenders and other exploiters, as a consequence of which they are thrown to abject poverty and continue their dependence on nature however little it may offer for their survival.

Ethnically the tribes of Orissa belong to the proto-Australoids and Dravidian groups and linguistically they either belong to the Mundari group of the Austric language family or they belong to the Dravidian linguistic groups. Most of the tribals of coastal plains have in course of time been transformed into caste groups while the hilly regions of western Orissa still contain large number of tribal communities. The tribes of north-western Orissa are exposed to greater amount of industrialization and mining developments while the tribes of south Orissa are still continuing their traditional life and they are comparatively less exposed to such opportunities. In the present paper illustrations will be chiefly given relating to the Kisans of north-western Orissa and the Sauras of South Orissa.

Features of the Traditional Tribal Economy

(a) Peasant Economy

The tribals of Orissa are by and large peasants. No doubt till the present day there are archaic tribes like the Juangs who have communal ownership of land through clan organization but production and consumption are regulated at the family level and all the characteristics of peasant life are fully seen amongst the tribes of Orissa. Yet the tribes of Orissa can be further classified under the following categories.

(1) Foodgatherers, hunters and those who have to depend on forest for their survival—The Mankindias of Sundargarh and Mayurbhanj, Koruwas of Sundargarh, Malhars of Dhenkanal and Keonjhar, Kolhas of Baudh-Phulbani etc. But their number is very insignificant.

(2) Shifting cultivators—Sauras, Juangs, Pauri Bhuyan, some sections of Khonds and other tribes of Koraput. They are in a transitional phase and combine food gathering and paddy cultivation along with Podu.

(3) Settled cultivators (or agricultural labourers) —Santals Oraons, Kisans, Kharias, Khonds, Parajas, Gadabas, Matia, Plain Bhuyans etc. belong to this group and they constitute majority of tribal population.

(4) Those who depend on mining, industries or specialised in some professions. The tribes of Sundargarh and Mayurbhanj belonging to Santal Oraon Kisans etc., belong to this group. Along with their agriculture they take up these new economic opportunities.

(5) Miscellaneous groups—consisting of service-holders, traders, workers of tea-gardens and artisans.

The above classification is by no means exclusive. Almost all tribal communities are peasants, live in villages and combine animal husbandry, poultry and different kinds of economic occupations to supplement their income. Thus barring a very few archaic peasants who depend on purely shifting cultivation others combine some amount of Podu cultivation

(Sweden cultivation) along with their settled agricultural practices. Whether one is a settled cultivator or Podu cultivator they depend and exploit the forest for their food gathering and hunting. Even service holders or artisans combine agricultural practices and food gaṭhering which shows that the tribal people are basically agriculturists and they try to adopt various means to fulfi their economic needs.

(b) Mode of Production Comparatively free from Monetized Economy

The tribal economy in India is long acquainted with money economy and acquisition of money, acts a powerful incentive in their economic life. Yet in the economic life of the tribes of Orissa, there are certain sectors which are still free from money economy though it is not true for all the tribal groups. Particularly those who depend on traditional Podu cultivation have retained to a great extent their mode of production free from the monetized economy. The land for such tribal groups is not a marketable commodity and any person belonging to the group has access to the resources such as land, forest or fishing and hunting places. These resources are owned jointly by the lineage or clan and are transmitted to the next generation through inheritance. After the introduction of Survey and Settlement the communal ownership of paddy land had been disrupted and such land has been marketable to some extent. But the traditional mode of production based on reciprocity still remains free from money economy. In tribal society whatever may be ownership of land, the productive operations are carried by the domestic group. Besides the domestic group, at the village level, there are reciprocal labour cooperatives which fulfil the requirements of individual families when the tasks are arduous and require swift execution. The presence of reciprocal labour cooperatives not only make the mode of production money-free but it also provides the tribal people to exploit the nature without the need of capital investment.

(c) Limited Scope for Development

The tribal communities live in areas where the scope of

agricultural development is rather limited. The hill slopes or undulating topography of tribal areas are unsuitable for paddy or wheat and mostly infertile and non-irrigated. The absence of irrigation makes tribal land further unfit for scientific cultivation and therefore the scope for improving tribal economy is rather remote unless extensive commercial and scientific steps are taken to introduce new cash crops and revolutionise their agricultural practices.

(d) Dependence on Market

In the present context there is rapid change in the economy and they have to depend heavily on markets for their very existence. Though the mode of production in tribal economy is comparatively free from money investment, soon after production the tribal people have to depend on market to dispose of their surplus products. Though tribal economy is primarily subsistence economy, to fulfil the demands of other economic necessities the tribal people have to sell their goods in the market. Since forest products have immense use in the outside world and some of the agricultural crops of tribal people have heavy demand in extensive areas, the traders rather penetrate into tribal pockets for these prized products. In the latter group will come various oilseeds, tamarind, beans, pulses, turmeric, etc. Which are the specialization of the tribal people while in the former group will come different varieties of medicinal products, materials useful for manufacture of chemical products oilseeds, honey, etc. Since long the tribals have been exposed to outside world through market and thus they have long since been integrated with money economy.

(e) The Economic Exploitation in Tribal Society

The tribal economy is stagnant for two reasons. Not only there is no scope for large-scale introducing innovations, but also they have been victims of exploitations for ages. During feudal days and clolonial rule the hill Chiefs, Mutha Patras, Bisoyees, Gountias and petty Government officials had exploited them systematically which broke the back-bone of their economy. On the other hand with the advent of modernization, money-lenders, liquor vendors, forest contractors and traders have been taking advantages of their ignorance and gullibility. Tribal lands have been alienated in large scale. With the courts, police and other modern institutions he has been put to most awkward position and thus he had been reduced to landless bonded labourer. Due to his economic insecurity he had to depend on his very exploiters for his mere existence.

Government Welfare Schemes to Improve Tribal People

During the colonial rule the tribals were exposed to outside world and new administrative policy restricted their economic pursuits. The forests were reserved, Podu cultivation was declared illegal and large number of Government officials, contractors, liquor vendors, money-lenders and traders made their inroads into tribal areas. In order to protect tribal people from exploitation and to improve their economic conditions so as to raise their standards of living, Government have taken many steps. All these measures are of two types:

(a) Overall planning at the macro-level and

(b) Specific tribal development schemes for the welfare of the tribal communities at the micro-level.

Large scale industrialization, agricultural development, communication, education and their welfare measures at the national level belong to the first category while specific projects for the welfare of tribal communities belong to the second category. Of course the second category is also within the broad framework of Five Year Plans but specific projects are made for quick development of tribal communities. The Community Development Blocks particularly, Tribal Development Blocks, Ashram and Sevashrama Schools, Tribal Development Agencies, Integrated Tribal Development Projects, Cooperative and LAMPS Societies, Small Farmers development projects are meant for tribal development work. Through all these welfare measures Government wants to eradicate all forms of exploitation from tribal societies, to ensure better income through just price for tribal products and to facilitate adoption of modern ways of life and avail new economic opportunities. It is difficult to assess the impact of all these projects on tribal economy and therefore I would present the economic conditions of two tribes referred to earlier.

The Kisan

The Kisan is a comparatively little known tribe of Orissa who speak a Dravidian language as their mother-tongue. Yet most of the Kisans are good in Oriya.

It is considered a branch of Oraons and their traditional folk-tales refer that they migrated to Orissa from Chota Nagpur of Bihar and from adjoining areas of Madhya Pradesh. Originally they were shifting cultivators and food gatherers but at present they have adopted paddy cultivation as the mainstay of their life. During the 19th century most of them were earth workers and agricultural labourers but slowly they have fanned out to different areas of Sundargarh and Sambalpur and have spread to Dhenkanal, Keonjhar and Balangir. They are known as Kuda and Mirdha in different areas. They have a passion for clearing forests and acquiring land and in the process they have successfully become land-owning cultivators in most of the areas. Though in some areas of Sundargarh and Sambalpur there are big land owners usually the Kisans are small farmers or work as agricultural labourers.

During post-Independence era most of the Kisans have improved remarkably. In 1963 a Kisan old man told me, "In old days we were doing very hard work but remained most of the days starved. In a family it was difficult to find four annas even. But at present in every family people get a square meal and one can get either one hundred or two hundred rupees easily. The same fields are there, the same amount of work we are doing now but we do not know due to which miracle our fortunes were transformed so quickly". Construction of Hirakud Dam and Rourkela Steel Factory and development of surrounding areas provided large scale employment opportunities for unskilled labourers. The sudden rise of prices of agricultural goods and opportunity to work in the collection of Kendu Leaves, road and building works, opportunities to work in mining areas of Lanjiberna, Biramitrapur and such other opportunities have transformed the economic life of the tribals of Sundargarh area. The Kisans are now interested to construct big houses and have better clothes and cosmetics. The pattern of food consumption and drinking of liquors remains unaltered ; yet Kisan mothers take an interest in educating their children. At present, rate of literacy is on the increase and along with it we find Kisan youths entering into private and Government organizations as school teachers, factory workers, Government officials and holding other types of jobs. Since they still retain agriculture as their most indispensable occupation they are improving due to rise of prices of agricultural goods. No doubt in some parts of Bamnda, the Kisans still depend on fruits and roots of the forest for their survival, the community on the whole has improved its economic conditions due to external market forces which help them to get better prices for their labour. No doubt still the poorer sections are exploited by moneylenders and petty officials though on the whole it is negligible in proportion to their overall economic development. Fortunately the Kisan society is well organised through clan and casts associations and they are bound to improve further in their struggle for economic uplift.

The Saura

The Sauras are the archaic sections of the great Savara tribe and they have retained to a large extent their traditional culture and economic habits. They live in the bordering hills of Koraput and Ganjam districts and follow shifting cultivation along with paddy cultivation. Describing the Saura economy Elwin writes:

> The Saoras are in many respects better off than the people of the plains. They sit in the lap of nature and she spoils them with a thousand simple gifts. Axe-cultivation ...gives splendid harvests The terraces so labouriously constructed give a rich return for the toil they demand.

But further Elwin writes in his colourful language :

> When harvest time is round, the Doms spend their days

> standing the Sauras threshing-floors scooping in their dues, filling their baskets with whatever they consider to be their rights. The Saoras threshing-floor in Ganjam is indeed one of the saddest places in India. This symbol of a life-time toil, this shrine into which Mother Earth pours her choicest gifts, is the scene of persistent and wholesale economic trickery and exploitation.

No doubt Elwin's description of Saora's economic well-being is slightly exaggerated. Even by the time Elwin did his field work in Koraput side, large number of Sauras were just living as serfs under mere well-to-do Sauras. But it is a fact that the Sauras have been exploited to a great extent by the businessmen mostly through their Dom agents. To add to this in the Ganjam side the existence of Muthadary System drained all their resources. Fortunately with the abolition of Muthadary and opening of fair prices and purchasing centres (T.D.C.C. stores at present) the rigour of exploitation has been reduced to a great extent. Yet a large number of the Sauras lead pathetic life living below the poverty line. The Sauras are neither educated like the tribals of Sundargarh and Mayurbhajja nor they have industrial zones which would provide better job opportunities. Previously large number of Sauras were going to work in the tea gardens of Assam. But in recent years they do not find the job opportunities in Assam very alluring. Most of the Sauras are underemployed and their traditional economic practices are very little altered. When demands of modern life require a heavy expenditure in terms of money the Sauras fail to earn sufficient to fulfil his present day requirements through adoption of improved agricultural practices. Now with the opening of roads and with better transport facilities the surplus agricultural products are making their way to urban centres putting the poorer sections in deplorable conditions. No doubt the Saura now get money through the sale of his agricultural products but he has to spend equally for his dress, liquor and other necessities of life. The Sauras have a rigorous life attuned to the agricultural cycles of shifting cultivation and paddy cultivation. So he cannot avail of the new economic opportunities in terms of temporary jobs on daily wage basis. On the other hand due to imposition of rigorous forest laws, his traditional economic activities are becoming restricted day by day. Yet the Sauras are struggling hard and with their simple and frugal life they are slowly improving their economic conditions and raising their standard of living.

Changing Economy

By and large both the tribes have improved their economic conditions after Independence. The ruthless exploitation of feudal days or colonial period has been substantially reduced if not completely annihilated. Abolition of Gountia system has given the scope for the Kisans to acquire more land while Sauras have got a new lease of life due to abolition of Muthadary.

During feudal days market forces could not have their full swing in tribal areas. Yet market had its extensions in interior areas. With the abolition of restrictions and infiltration of all types of traders there is scope for the tribal people for entering into larger market economy. In the present context extension of market is not an unmixed blessing. Through marketing, there is large scale exploitation and pauperization of tribal areas. But it is inevitable and the tribal people should learn how to adjust with the new economy.

With planning, new economic opportunities are available at the doors of tribal people. But lack of education make them only unskilled labourers. Due to their special advantages and greater mobility and better educational facilities the Kisans are better adjusted to new situations.

Yet both the tribes are still pursuing their traditional agricultural parctices. Though they are able to earn more amount of money due to rise in prices of agricultural goods, they have not learnt how to modernize or improve their economic conditions. The Sauras still use human energy to a great extent and combine the use of animal energy sometimes. Though the Kisans are using animal energy, in agriculture, they cannot reach the level of the Kulta, the Agaria or even Telis in agricultural practices.

Scientific agriculture is not yet adopted by both the tribes. None uses pumps sets for irrigation nor electricity is used for agricultural operations.

Failure of Government

On the whole the tribal economy is still in static position and the traditional technology and agricultural practices are still chiefly practised. This may provide them with bare necessities of life but cannot raise standard of living. No doubt by virtue of their hard labour on traditional lines they are in a better position from their earlier stages yet they have not got any benefit from modern technology. If their standard of living is to be raised, if they should be free from starvation, illiteracy and disease much more concerted effort is necessary. Conservation of every drop of water and surface soil, construction of innumerable water reservoirs and fitting these with pump sets, introduction of exotic crops, afforestation, development of pasture lands, imparting training in better methods of agriculture through formal and non-formal education, introducing small scale industries at the village level, establishment of regional research centres with extension services are the few items which should be attempted with zeal and sincerity. At the present stage all the plannings and their executions are carried by bureaucracy. But the Government servants only know how to prepare projects and they spend money perfunctorily. The net result is that the tribal people remain in the same stage of underdevelopment though they have comparatively improved their conditions from the days of colonial period. It is high time to train tribal leaders and entrust them with the responsibility of rebuilding the tribal economy on scientific lines. For this there should be large scale imparting of education that will train them how to adopt innovations and bring revolutionary changes in the tribal economy through introduction of scientific technology.

The tribes of Orissa never posed a threat to the National integration. Living in the mainland from time immemorial they have adopted culture and traditions of larger society to a gerat extent while retaining their own cultural identity. It is therefore necessary to consider first how far they maintain separatist tendency before discussing the ways for their integration within Indian nationality.

My presumption is that in the traditional Indian society the tribal people were better integrated with larger society and there developed disruption only after modernization particularly after the beginning of the colonial rule. Due to various historic forces the tribal people are now searching their separate identity and retracing their foot-steps. Sometimes we fail to visualize the close relationship of tribal people with their neighbours and unnecessarily attribute tribals as having separatist tendency.

Both in academic discussions and at official levels the tribal people are considered those people who have remained segregated from the mainstream of Indian population. But despite their ignorance, in the past, tribals had been playing heroically their roles and it would be unjust to assume that they had no historic role in the development of Indian culture.

In the present context the tribal people are considered minorities. But in our democratic set-up we have failed to solve any of their problems by simply attributing them the minority status.

At this juncture, it is high time to consider the place of tribals in the traditional Indian civilization.

In traditional Indian policy the state-tribe interaction was rather smooth and peaceful as dynasty after dynasty emerged out of the tribal base in an orthogenetic process. It is reported that large number of dynasties in Orissa emerged from different ethnic groups such as "Sailodbhaba" from the Sauras "Bhanja Puranas" from Bhumijas or "Gondram" kings from the Gonds. Some of the coronation rituals in feudatory states indicate as the survivals of the same orthogenetic process of state-tribe interaction. At the time of coronation of the Raja of Keonjhar he had to sit on the lap of a Juang Chief while a Bhuyan chief had to give Tika on his forehead as a mark of his legitimacy to the royal throne. The Kalahandi Raja at the time of his coronation in olden days had to marry Khond lady who was subsequently maintained by the State. All these rituals indicate close relation of former Raja with local tribal groups. In the state policy the tribal groups were allowed to pursue their styles and traditions with tribal chiefs or heads and the administration was mostly indirectly being carried by natural local leaders who assumed legitimacy according to local traditions. On the occasions of either invasion or defence tribal militia had been playing their heroic roles in the past.

The Oriya Rajas along with their militia sometimes were only a minority, but since there was no cleavage between tribals and non-tribals there was smooth process of acculturation that led to assimilation in tribal areas. Not only the tribal deities were syncretized as Hindu gods the Rajas had been playing the important role of religious heads amongst tribal communities.

With the disruption of earlier state-tribe interaction and with the introduction of foreign rules and regulations in the tribal areas, with the suppression of tribal communities by depriving them from using any weapons for their self-protection the tribal people became minorities in their home-land and had to play a subordinate role before a handful of Government officials. Suppression of the Khonds on the pretext of removing human sacrifice, transporting and hanging large number of the Saoras the alien rulers created a fear complex and a sense of inferiority in the minds of the tribals from which they were not fully free in spite of paternalistic policy of British Government.

Later throughout British period we find the exploitation of tribal people by non-tribals which manifested sporadically in the form of revolts such as Khonds' revolt against Kultas in Sambalpur and Saura revolts against the Panos which occurred several times.

Despite such sporadic disruptions the tribes of Orissa had been loyal to their local Rajas throughout the British period and were identifying themselves as subjects of particular Rajas.

This situation clearly shows that though some of the tribes of Orissa are still maintaining their distinct culture and language they do not consider themselves completely separate from the local non-tribal people. Yet due to politicization process, missionary activities and political movements such as the activities of Jharkhand Party and nativistic movements such as revival of 'Sarna religion' amongst the Santals and Mundas sometimes primordial sentiments are aroused that may weaken the forces of integration. We may therefore think seriously how to bring integration amongst tribal communities which cannot be ignored by any means particularly considering their size in the population of Orissa.

Again in exploring the ways of integration I feel we should learn from history how the Rajas of old could integrate tribal population in spite of their distinct religion, language and culture.

Yet while taking the model from traditional Indian policy, some amount of caution is necessary considering the differences in situations. The old Raja had direct and personal contact with tribal chiefs and he played his multi-variegated role more successfully when the society was simple. Monarchical powers curbed the independence and freedom of expression on certain occasions which were definitely against the democratic norms. Yet we have to explore our past to face the challenges of modern age.

In ancient India though monarchy was prevalent the real power was devolved on the local chief who actually wielded power but again he had to pass on such power to village headmen who acted both as the representative of the people and the Raja. Thus the local administration in the ancient India was regulated on democratic lines where different ethnic groups represented and participated keeping in view the local problems and difficulties. Living in the same environment and facing the same types of problems along with others and working under their accredited popular leaders the tribal groups could identify themselves with their Raja and his territory. In a country like India if the local level administration can effectively fulfil the local needs, if real powers are transferred to local leaders, if tribals are given the full freedom to manifest their own genius, it will create situation for the smooth solution of tribal problems and their integration with the local society will be complete, provided the local units act with full sincerity and the majority groups get scope to act as majority in their own locality. The local level administration should run all welfare activities and should educate and appoint its youths in local organizations which are geared to the larger organization of the state and the nation. If the problems are solved at the local level by the genius of local leaders guided by the experts at the Government level, if the tribals get scope in building their own local institutions which would bring prosperity to them, perhaps national integration will be built on finer grounds which would ensure peace and prosperity at the local level and assure greatness of the country at the national level.

In the present situation through sub-plans, Panchayat Samiti and Gram Panchayat, Government is trying hard to introduce decentralised administration but unfortunately in most of these organizations, the active participation of tribal people is minimum. No doubt with the creation of above institutions infrastructure is built for local level administration throughout the country but unfortunately most of these institutions are neither very effective nor successful in implementing their objectives.

In the present from of decentralized administrative units, somehow the traditional tribal leaders are eliminated or have lost their dominance. With introduction of Gram Panchayat the traditional village organization has lost its power and prestige. It is high time that traditional village organizations should be recognized and all natural leaders at the village level should be entrusted with development works.

No doubt the economic development is the first and foremost duty of the Government in the tribal areas. A thorough economic survey should be made in all tribal areas and people should be given proper guidance as how to improve their e conomic conditions. Not only the hereditary right of tribal people over their land should be safeguarded but also the tribal youths should be trained in new types of skills and they should be engaged in local developmental works.

For any developmental work, raising the educational and intellectual standard is the first and foremost. The present form of educational process is long, tedious and quite frustrating for tribal youths. With a view to getting quick results there should be an attempt to revive traditional culture, and development of tribal languages and folk-lores through non-formal education. With the revival of their culture and tradition the tribal people may feel more enthusiastic to further develop their own cultural norms and traditions. The State level Tribal Institutes, Cultural Academy and Educational Department should jointly cooperate to give concrete shape to such cultural regeneration.

APPENDIX
(Ch. 10-Figures)

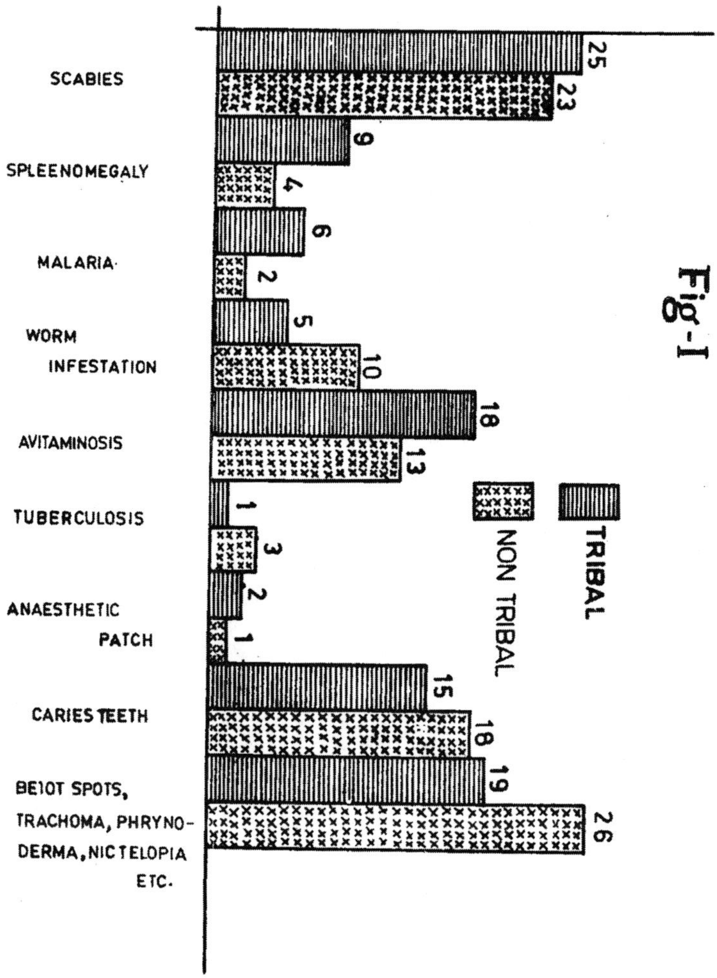
SCABIES
25
23
SPLEENOMEGALY
9
4
MALARIA
6
2
WORM INFESTATION
5
10
AVITAMINOSIS
18
13
TUBERCULOSIS
1
3
ANAESTHETIC PATCH
2
1
CARIES TEETH
15
18
BEIOT SPOTS, TRACHOMA, PHRYNODERMA, NICTELOPIA ETC.
19
26
TRIBAL
NON TRIBAL

Fig-I

Fig-A
DISEASE OF CHILDREN
(5 TO 15 YEARS)

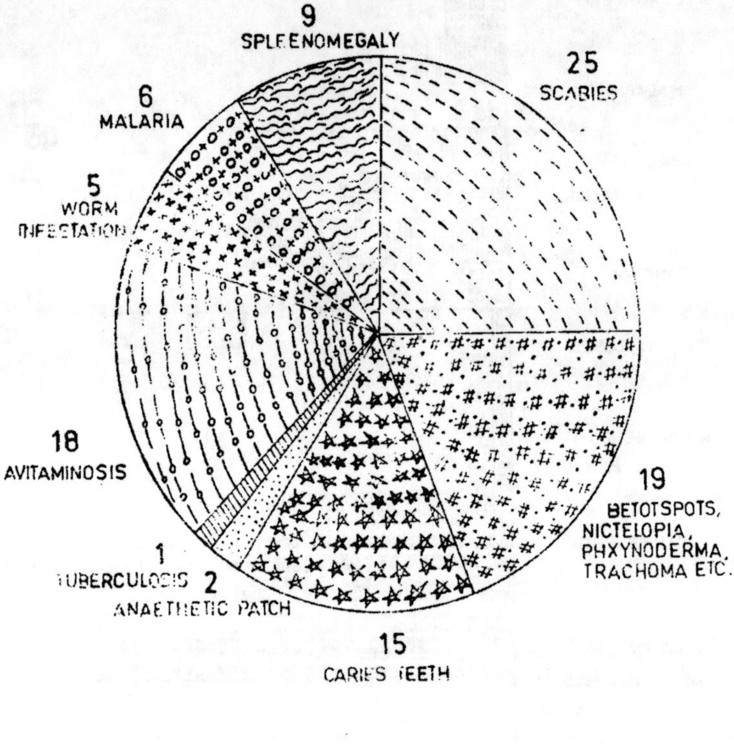

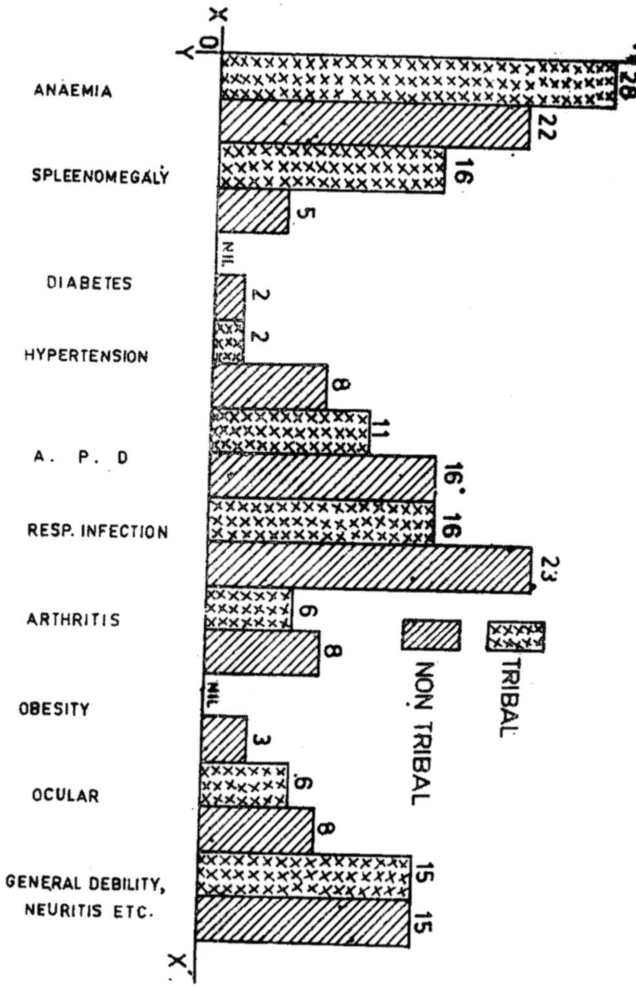

ANAEMIA
SPLEENOMEGALY
DIABETES
HYPERTENSION
A. P. D
RESP. INFECTION
ARTHRITIS
OBESITY
OCULAR
GENERAL DEBILITY, NEURITIS ETC.
TRIBAL
NON TRIBAL
X
O
Y
X'
Y'
28
22
16
5
NIL
2
2
8
11
16
16
23
6
8
NIL
3
6
8
15
15

Fig II

Fig-B
DISEASE PATTERN IN ADULTS

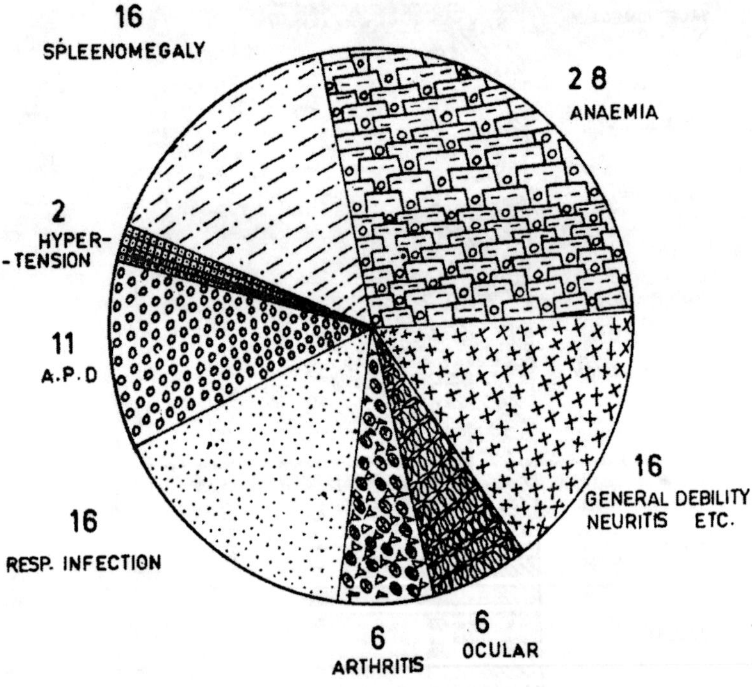

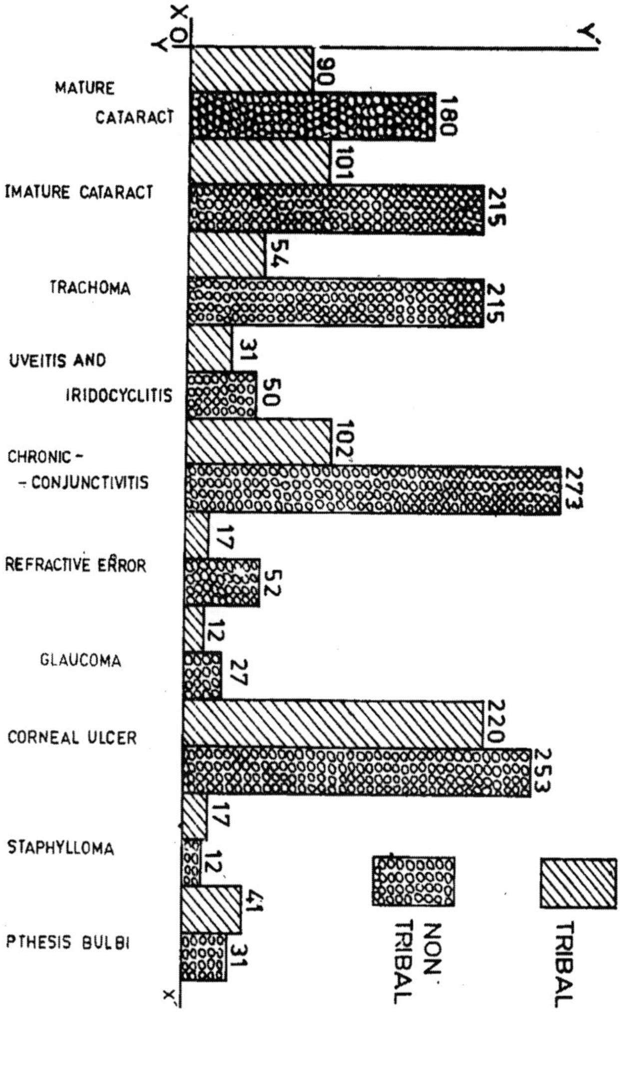
X
O
Y
Y'
X'
MATURE CATARACT
90
180
IMATURE CATARACT
101
215
TRACHOMA
54
215
UVEITIS AND IRIDOCYCLITIS
31
50
CHRONIC - - CONJUNCTIVITIS
102
273
REFRACTIVE ERROR
17
52
GLAUCOMA
12
27
CORNEAL ULCER
220
253
STAPHYLLOMA
17
12
PTHESIS BULBI
41
31
NON TRIBAL
TRIBAL

Fig-III

Fig-C
EYE DISEASE

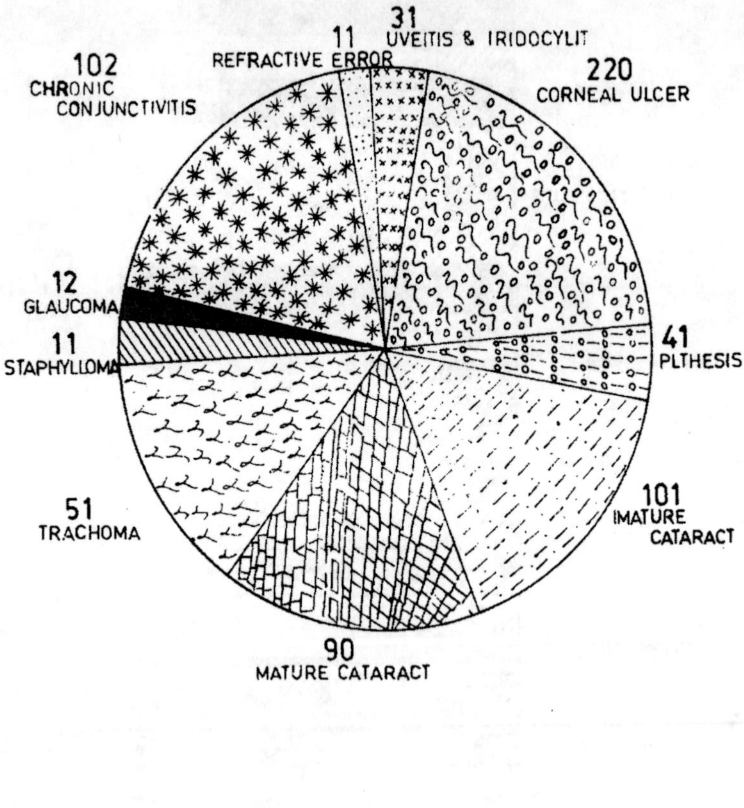

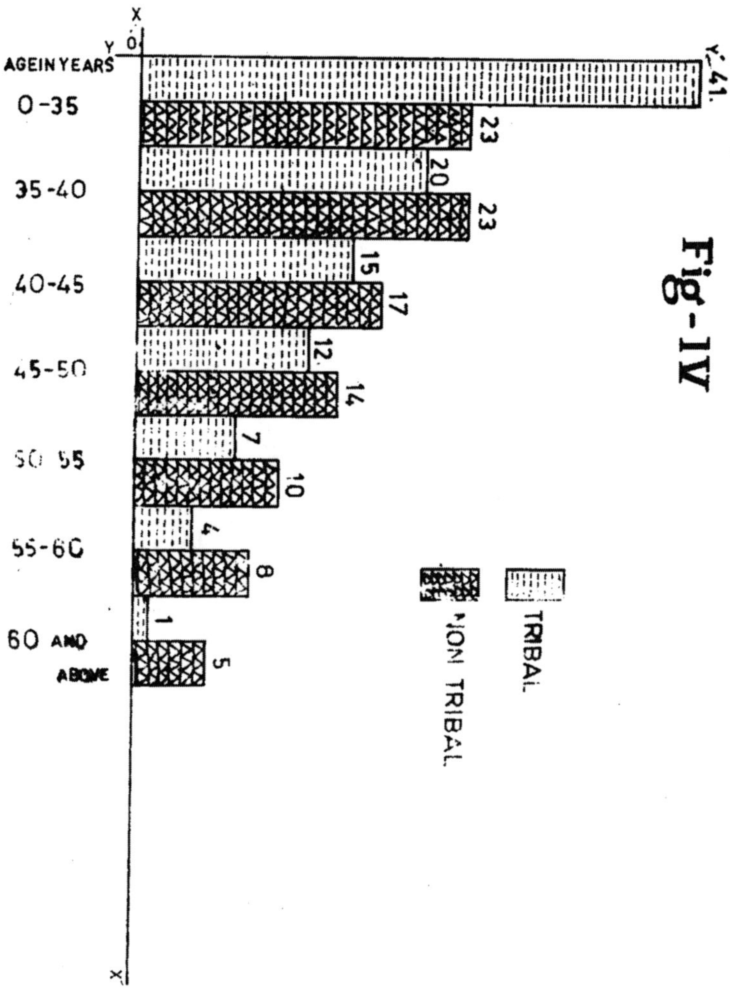

AGE IN YEARS
0-35
35-40
40-45
45-50
50-55
55-60
60 AND ABOVE
41
23
20
23
15
17
12
14
7
10
4
8
1
5
TRIBAL
NON TRIBAL

Fig-IV

Fig-D
AGE IN YEARS
(LONGEVITY)

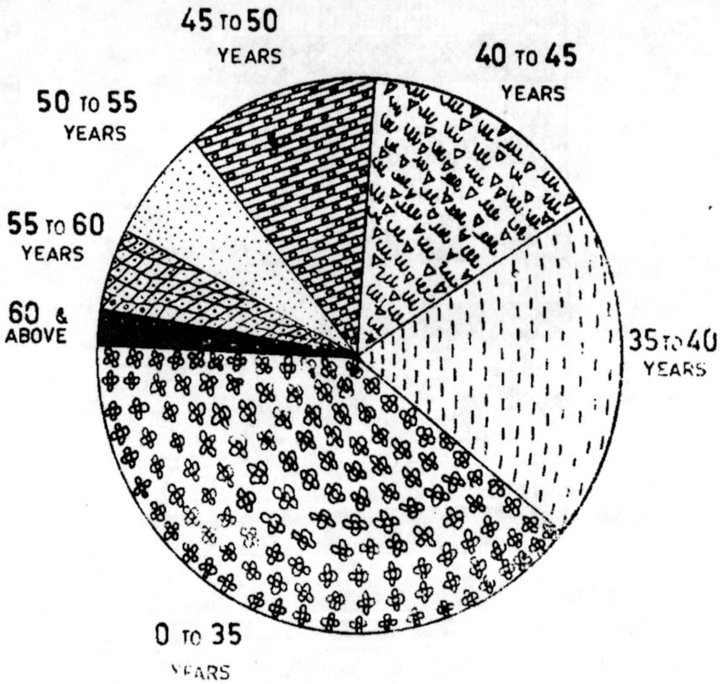

INDEX

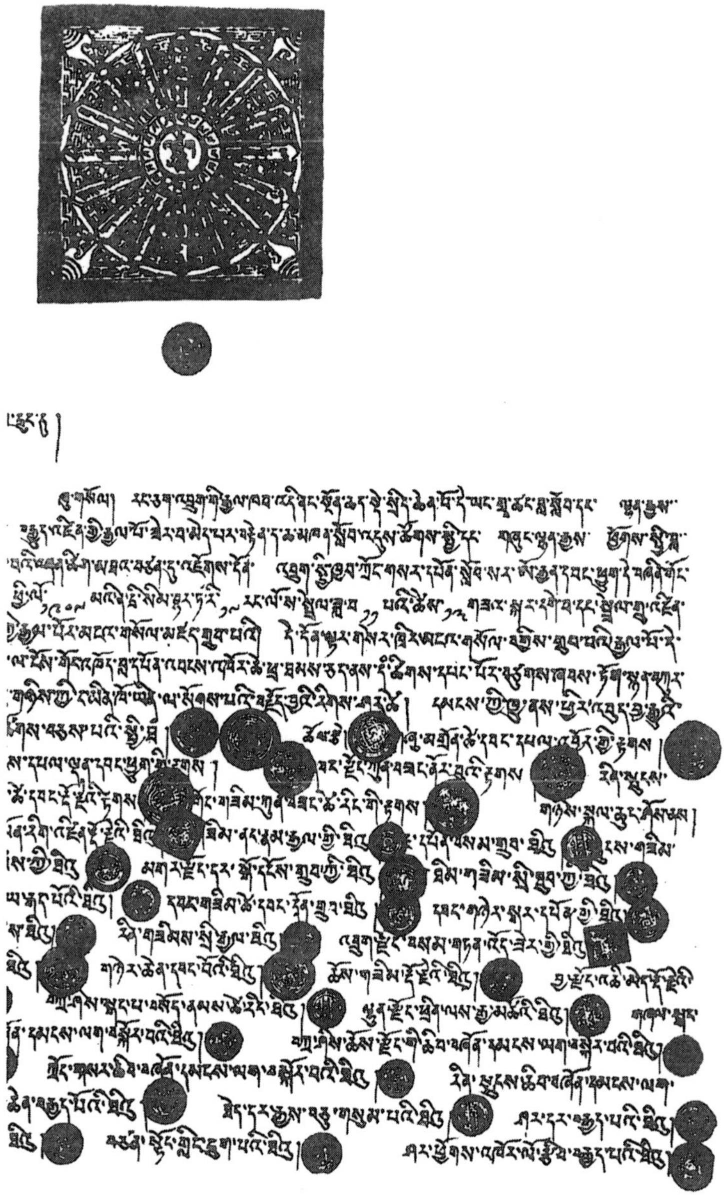

D AT POONAKHA AT THE INSTALLATION OF SIR UGYEN WANG-CHUK
AS MAHARAJA OF BHUTAN, 1907

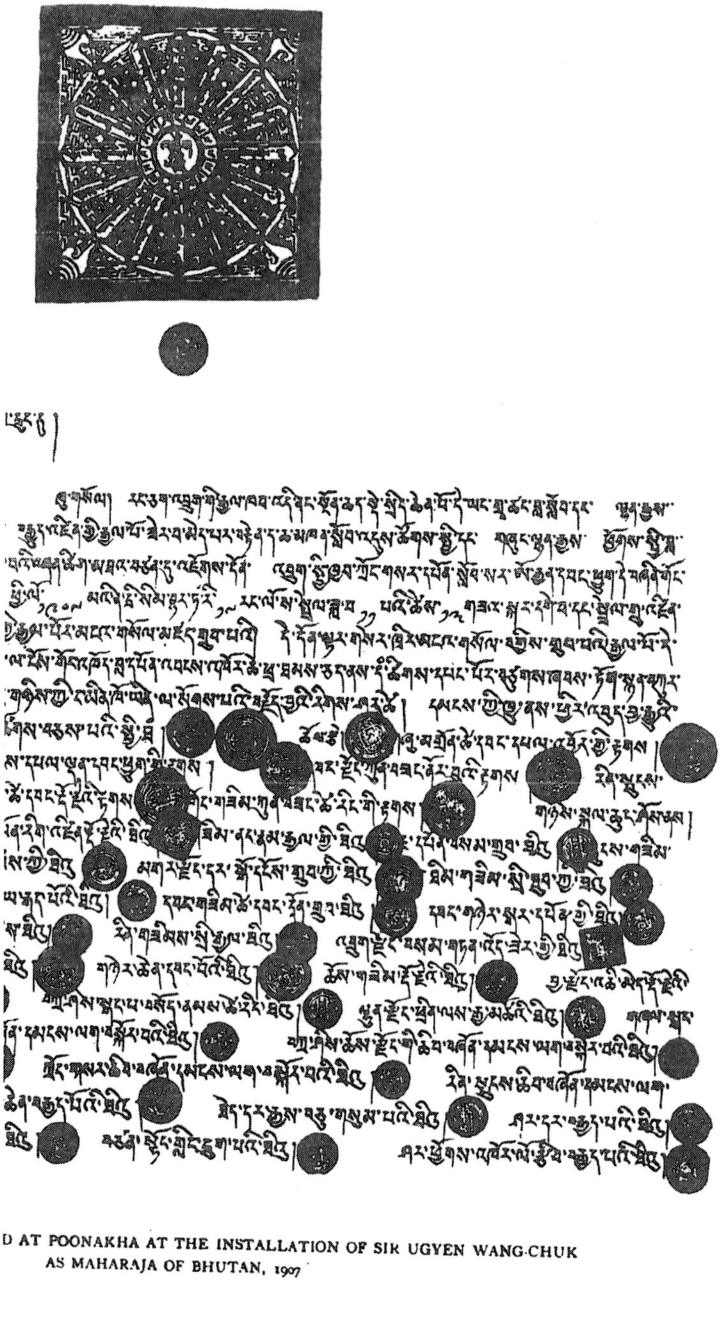

D AT POONAKHA AT THE INSTALLATION OF SIR UGYEN WANG-CHUK AS MAHARAJA OF BHUTAN, 1907